AMAZING REAL LIFE COINCIDENCES

D0460218

AMAZING REAL LIFE COINCIDENCES

DOUGLAS COLLIGAN

SCHOLASTIC INC.

New York Toronto London Auckland Sydney

ISBN 0-590-31275-8

12 11 10 9 8 7 6 5   0 1 2 3/9

Printed in the U.S.A.   01

Coincidences of Life or Death

Just as you're thinking about a friend, the phone rings. It's that same friend calling you. You click on your radio as you're humming your favorite song and hear the same tune being played. You walk into a strange room and get the spooky feeling you've been there before. Then you realize you saw the room last night, in a dream.

Coincidences. That's what most people call odd events like these. And life is full of big and small coincidences. Although all kinds of experts have spent years trying to figure them out, no one really knows why they happen. A coincidence has a way of suddenly appearing and just as suddenly disappearing, amazing and confusing everyone involved. It's one mystery of life that will probably always be unsolved.

Most coincidences come and go and are soon forgotten. But the one that everyone remembers the best is the one that means the difference between life and death. Sometimes, for no particular reason, one or more strange things will happen to people that will end up saving their lives. As you will see, sometimes that thing is a mysterious voice that seems to come out of the air; or a vague, sudden impulse that seizes a person; or an eerie dream that haunts someone for years; or it can be a whole series of seemingly insignificant events that have a peculiar lifesaving spell, such as the night the lives of 15 people were saved simply because they were late.

One winter evening back in the 1950's there was a non-disaster in the small town of Beatrice, Nebraska. A non-disaster is the kind of accident where no one is killed, no one is hurt, no one even gets rumpled or dirty. What happened was a church in town was totally demolished by a tremendous explosion, the result of a faulty furnace. At the time of the explosion, 7:30 in the evening, there was no one in the church or even near it, and fortunately none of the church members or anyone else in town was hurt.

It doesn't sound like much of a story, does it? It is. A few weeks later it was national news and later on the story of the demolished church in Beatrice was made into a television drama. The reason for this attention was coincidence, or more exactly, a series of very simple coincidences that saved the lives of 15 men and women.

To appreciate the story you have to know a little bit about the night of the explosion and those 15 people, who were all members of the church

Contents

choir. Once a week the members of the choir would get together for a practice session. The evening the church was obliterated by the explosion was one of them. The people in the choir enjoyed practice and they had one unwritten rule that absolutely no one ever broke without a very good reason: always be on time for practice.

Everyone in the choir took practice very seriously and each was extra careful about getting to the church on the dot of 7:20 on practice nights. Since choir practice couldn't begin until everyone was present, the members quietly discouraged anyone who wasn't punctual from joining.

What was genuinely strange about the church explosion in Beatrice was that at the time the church blew up, 7:30 in the evening, not one of the 15 choir members was inside the building, even though it was a practice night. Every one of them had been late for practice. Although it seemed possible that one or two people might have been late, it was hard to believe that not one of these 15 punctual people showed up on that one night. But that's exactly what happened.

Why was this? Was there some special force that kept them all away? If you had been able to follow around each choir member that night, you would have seen nothing unusual going on. There were no ghostly warnings to stay away from the church. No weird premonitions about a disaster. Just a lot of routine delays. In one case a young couple had to skip practice at the last minute when their baby-sitter got sick and couldn't show up. Another member of the choir couldn't get his car started and had to call up someone else for a ride. As a result both people were late. Others were delayed for equally ordinary reasons; but when you put all these ordinary delays together, you get one big, extraordinary coincidence. Although all 15 people were trying hard to keep that 7:20 appointment, each was just late enough to miss being killed in that freak explosion. It was one of the best non-disasters the town ever had.

Lifesaving coincidences can even happen to people who don't care if they live or die. During the winter of 1977, there was a man in New York City who decided he didn't want to live anymore. It was a little less than two weeks before Christmas, and he was tremendously depressed. He decided he was going to end it all and jump off the top of the Empire State Building, which is 102 stories high.

He got on an elevator with a crowd of tourists and rode up to the observation deck up near the top. When no one was looking, he climbed over the railing, hesitated a second or two, then jumped. Just as he did a powerful wind came whipping by. It was so strong it actually picked the man up and blew him back onto the building. He landed on a ledge just a few feet below where he jumped off. If he had jumped just a little sooner or a little bit later he would have been lying dead on the sidewalk 102 stories below instead of sitting alive and well on a building ledge.

As he sat there thinking about this, he decided that maybe suicide wasn't such a good idea after all. All of a sudden he didn't feel like jumping anymore. He inched his way over to the nearest window and timidly tapped on the glass. A totally surprised secretary opened the window and let him back inside. Because of that lifesaving wind which just happened to blow at the right time, he was given a second chance.

Coincidence expert Arthur Koestler tells about another attempt at suicide that was foiled because of an equally lucky coincidence. It happened at a subway platform in the city of London one chilly day in November, 1971. A young man, a talented architect, had decided to kill himself by jumping in front of the next train that rolled into the station.

In a few minutes he heard the faint rumble of an approaching train and inched up to the edge of the platform where he watched the subway's headlights reflecting off the tracks. As it got closer, he took one last deep breath to calm himself and, just as it rounded the curve, he jumped.

The engineer saw the young man jump and instinctively reached for the brake. Even as he did it he knew it was too late. There was no way he would be able to stop in time. The front car had already begun to roll over the man lying there on the tracks. Just when it seemed as though it were going to crush him completely the train screeched to a stop. The engineer stood there amazed. He knew his brake hadn't stopped the train. But what did?

Firemen and ambulance attendants scrambled to the scene. They couldn't believe how close the man had come to getting killed. He was squeezed so tightly under the first car that they had to get special equipment to jack up the train and free him. The man was badly bruised and had several broken bones, but he was alive. He was rushed to the hospital where the doctors said that with a little care, he would survive.

In the meantime subway officials had arrested a man on the same train. They charged him with pulling the emergency brake, which locks all the brakes on the train, for no reason. They were planning to take him to court when they discovered that it was the emergency brake and not the engineer's brake which stopped the train and saved the young architect's life. Once they heard this they quickly dropped all charges.

The strange thing about the incident is why that man pulled the brake. He was much too far back in the train to see anyone jumping off the subway platform, yet he managed to pull the brake at just the right time. If he had waited a second or two longer, it would have been too late. If he couldn't see anyone, why did he pull the brake? When subway officials asked him, he couldn't give them a satisfactory explanation. All he knew, he said, was that he felt an uncontrollable urge to do it. He didn't find out about saving someone's life until long after the accident.

The mysterious urges that set these lifesaving coincidences in motion can occasionally be a special signal, according to Arthur Koestler. He was told a weird story from an old retired miner who said a mysterious voice once saved his life. When he was about 23 years old, the old man said, he was assigned to work in what was called a "room" in the coal mine. It was just a hollowed-out area carved into the side of a rich vein of coal hundreds of feet below ground.

It was grim, lonely work. Each room was only big enough for one man, whose job was to hack large chunks of coal from the wall, load them into a cart and, when the cart was full, push it down a long skinny passage about three feet high to a main tunnel. There a man driving a small tractor would hitch up the full cart and drop off another empty one to be taken back to the room.

Although the passageway was the only route to and from the room, there were other smaller openings off to either side of the room. They were ventilation tunnels, barely large enough for a man to squeeze through.

One day the miner had dropped off a full cart in the main tunnel, but since there was no tractor in sight, he decided to go back to the room and wait until one did show up. He had crawled through the narrow little passageway and was just stepping into the room when he heard the tractor driver yell out that he had an empty cart waiting for him. He was about to head back toward the main tunnel when he heard a voice shout, "Stop!" Without even thinking, he froze. A few seconds later the same voice commanded, "Quick, go! Go!"

He dove into the ventilation tunnel to his right and crawled through it as fast as he could. In a few seconds he had reached another room. (This one was abandoned because it was all worked out.) A few seconds after he got there, he heard a loud crack and then a roar as tons of rock caved in on the room where he had just been working. The blast of air from the cave-in was so strong it blew out his miner's lamp. By following the light from other miners' lamps he was able to pick his way through the dust and the blackness and get out.

The man was never able to find out who it was who shouted to him. It wasn't a voice he recognized and, although it didn't seem possible, it came from a place where no one could have possibly been standing — right over his head. There was nothing there but the ceiling of the room, which was hundreds of feet of solid rock. Yet it was from there the man said he heard the voice, and whoever or whatever it was knew what he was talking about. Those split-second commands saved the miner's life. The man took the warning very seriously. He never went back to that mine.

For some people lifesaving coincidences like this can be more than just a one-time event. There are a few people who somehow seem to lead a charmed life, always sidestepping danger and death at the last minute. One of these was Dr. Victor Heiser, a famous surgeon in the early 1900's. Many times in his life he just breezed by death and disaster without even getting his hair mussed.

One day he was traveling north by train and decided to stop in New York City overnight. He made reservations in one of the city's better establishments, the Murray Hill Hotel, and was about to sign in when he was handed a telegram. It said he was needed in Toronto as soon as possible to perform a critical operation. He immediately cancelled his room and hopped on the next train heading for Canada. That evening while he was traveling north, there was a huge explosion in one of the subway tunnels in New York. It went off directly underneath the Murray Hill Hotel, causing tremendous damage and killing a number of guests in the hotel. One of those killed was a man who stayed in the room Dr. Heiser would have occupied if he hadn't gotten that telegram.

On another occasion he was asked to travel to Mexico by the U.S. government during a particularly dangerous time. There was a revolution going on in Mexico. Travel was difficult and risky, especially if you weren't a Mexican. Rebels and bandits roamed the country pretty much doing as they pleased. Heiser found that so many of the train routes were blocked or blown up, that the only way he could get to Mexico City was by a long, complicated train trip through some wild country.

He had bought his ticket and was already in Texas ready to leave when he received another one of those lucky telegrams, telling him to wait a few more days. The next morning his train took off without him. Halfway through its trip south, it was stopped by a band of rebels who went through the train car by car, pulling everyone off who was not a Mexican. Then they lined up all these people and shot them.

A year or two later the lucky Dr. Heiser, who liked to travel quite a bit, was in Burma and had to go to the city of Mandalay. He went to the train station to buy tickets but, just as he approached the ticket window, he decided that he liked staying where he was. He had some time to kill and decided to wait a couple of extra days before going on to Mandalay. He explained to the confused ticket seller, "I'm sorry but I don't think I'll buy the ticket just now. Perhaps in a day or two."

When the train pulled out of the station that day Dr. Heiser was not on it. Once again his luck worked. The train bounced off the tracks a few miles down the track, injuring hundreds of passengers.

There is at least one other near-miss story told

about Dr. Heiser that happened to him when he was in India. While visiting a friend who was an American diplomat there, he received one of his many telegrams telling him he was needed in Damascus. Dr. Heiser was about to make plans to travel there by train, when his friend said that it wasn't really necessary. As it happened the friend also was traveling to Damascus, only not by train but in a chauffeur-driven car. He had room for another passenger and said he would welcome the company.

Dr. Heiser thanked his friend for the offer but said he would go by train just the same. He did and had a quiet ride to Damascus. For the diplomat the trip was a little more exciting. Partway to Damascus the car was attacked by bandits. They fired a few shots at the car before it raced away. One of the shots struck and killed someone who had accepted the diplomat's generous offer of a ride. That person was sitting in the same place where Dr. Heiser would have been had he gone.

No one knows if Dr. Heiser could feel danger ahead of time or whether he just knew by instinct what was the safest thing to do. There are people who can feel danger approaching and sometimes are even able to see it long before it happens. One famous case discovered by a psychic expert named Louisa Rhine had to do with a young mother, her baby, and the creaky old house where they lived.

One night after she went to bed, the mother had

a terrifying dream that during the night a sudden, fierce wind started shaking the old house. The wind was so strong it loosened an enormous chandelier hanging from the ceiling in her infant daughter's room. Eventually the chandelier worked itself free and dropped down on the baby's crib.

This woke the woman with a start. It took a few seconds to realize she had been dreaming and nothing had actually happened. She listened. It was perfectly quiet outside. There wasn't even the hint of a wind. Still, she couldn't get the dream out of her mind. To reassure herself, she slipped into her child's room for a peek. Her baby lay there sleeping quietly.

She was about to leave when she took one last look at the chandelier. It was huge, she thought. Although she felt a little silly doing it, she rolled her baby's crib from under the chandelier off to one side of the room. Then she went back to bed.

A few hours later a freak wind came out of nowhere. It slammed into the house, rattling everything inside. It was blowing so hard it woke the woman up, just in time to hear the chandelier come crashing down in the room next door on the empty spot on the floor where her baby had been.

If we can believe what happened to a Captain McPherson, then there also have been times when people have been able to feel danger to people they've never even seen before. One night in 1828, McPherson's ship was in the middle of the crossing between Europe and Newfoundland. He was in his cabin, writing in the ship's log. As he sat at his desk he saw through an open door somebody moving around in the cabin next to him. Since no one was using the cabin on that trip, he was a little bit curious about who was there.

When he looked up he saw a man standing back in the shadows, staring at him. There was still enough light to see what the man looked like and McPherson could tell that it was no one from the crew and was not one of his few passengers. The man must be a stowaway, the captain thought. He jumped up from his desk and ran into the room. There was no one there. There was no way the man could have escaped or hidden in the small cabin. Just the same he had somehow managed to disappear.

It was late and he was tired. The captain thought maybe his eyes were playing tricks on him, until he turned to leave the cabin. Scrawled on the wall in shaky letters was a four-word message: "Steer to the northwest." He blinked and looked again. Unlike the man, the message did not disappear.

The captain was not a superstitious man and did not believe in anything such as ghosts, but there was something about the mysterious message that impressed him. He sent instructions to the bridge to change the course of the ship, heading it northwest. A few hours later he was called up to the bridge. Just ahead, drifting aimlessly on the ocean, was what was left of a ship that had been badly smashed up in a storm. It was half-flooded and on the verge of sinking. A search party went aboard to see if anyone was still alive.

They found only one man. When he was carried aboard the captain immediately recognized him. He was the man he had seen in the cabin. When the man had recovered well enough to speak, the captain sat down and talked to him. The sailor said his ship had been drifting for days. Without food and without hope of being rescued, the man did little else but sleep. He lay in a deep sleep for most of that night and had a dream that McPherson's ship was coming out of the night to rescue him. The next thing he knew some people were carrying him onto another ship. There was nothing in his dream about writing a message on the wall of the cabin, although when it was shown to him, he had to admit that it did look a little like his writing. How it got there he didn't really know.

The prize for the eeriest danger warning would have to go to the story told about a British aristocrat named Lord Dufferin who lived in England in the late 1800's. Unlike the other tales about warnings of danger, his covers a time span of many years between the warning and the danger itself.

The story starts in the 1880's when Dufferin was visiting the estate of some friends in Ireland. He had trouble sleeping one night, and found himself sitting upright in bed wide awake. Feeling a little restless, he climbed out of bed and wandered over to his bedroom window which overlooked the vast front lawn of his friend's estate.

The moon was so bright that night he could see almost as well as if it were in the middle of the day. He happened to spot a man dragging a long, narrow box, which he half-carried on his back, across the lawn. Lord Dufferin stepped outside and walked toward the man. He asked why he was working so hard so late at night. The man didn't say anything but looked out from under the shadow of the box. He was repulsive-looking. He had two glistening black eyes which he fixed on Dufferin, and he twisted his dried-up face into a horrible, leering grin. Then he stooped back under the load of his long box, which looked very much like a coffin, and shuffled off into the darkness.

The next morning Lord Dufferin asked who that ugly little man was who was dragging a box around in the night. None of his friends seemed to have any idea of what he was talking about. They said no one worked for them or even lived in the area who looked like that. Dufferin never saw the man again during his visit, and he eventually forgot about the whole incident.

Ten years later he and a friend were invited to a party at the Grand Hotel in Paris, one of the most luxurious hotels in the city. Since the party was being held on the fifth floor, they strolled over to the elevator and were about to get on, when Lord Dufferin stepped back and pulled his friend back with him.

The young man was puzzled by Dufferin's odd move. There was more than enough room for the two of them on the elevator but to humor Dufferin his friend stayed and watched idly as the elevator operator, a strange-looking little man with a grotesque face and black glistening eyes, slid the door shut.

Dufferin, in the meantime, had rushed over to the registration desk and was asking the clerk about the man working on the elevator. At that moment there were loud screams and a sickening crash. The cable on the elevator had snapped just as it reached the fifth floor. In a matter of seconds it dropped to the bottom of the shaft, killing everyone on it. If he had gotten on the elevator, Dufferin would have been among the dead.

After the accident Lord Dufferin was more curious than ever about who that man was. He never found out. No one ever came to claim the man's body, and when the hotel checked its files it couldn't find any record of him. No one had any idea why that strange man was running the elevator, no one, that is, except Dufferin, who saw him as an omen of death.

2

In the Nick of Time

The mother probably hadn't turned her back for more than 30 seconds when her small son, only a year old, spotted the open window and climbed up on the sill. Even on the first story of an ordinary house this would have been a dangerous thing to do, but the situation was worse than that. This window was in an apartment and that apartment was up on the 14th floor of a tall building. The mother heard her small son squealing with delight and turned around. He was reaching out, trying to touch a bird that was flying by. She raced to the window but it was too late. Her baby lost his balance and fell.

At that same time a man named Jack Figlock was walking by the building preoccupied with his own thoughts. He of course had no idea about the horrible thing that had just happened to the little boy . . . yet. Suddenly he felt like something or someone hit him hard on the back, so hard he was knocked flat on his face. Completely dazed he looked up and saw someone else lying on the ground next to him. It was the little boy who had fallen out of the window. Figlock just happened to be walking under that open apartment window when the baby fell out and landed right on top of him. His being in that particular spot on the sidewalk at that particular second saved the baby's life.

Everyone naturally mentioned how lucky it was that Figlock walked by that building in the nick of time and acted as a kind of human safety net for the little kid. Those kinds of things happen only once in a lifetime. Or do they?

A year later Figlock was in the same city (Detroit), was walking by the same building, and suddenly found himself sprawled all over the sidewalk again. He looked up and — that's right — there was *another* baby lying on the ground nearby. This one, strangely enough, also lived on the 14th floor of that same apartment building (different apartment) and had also managed to fall out of an open window. Just like the first one that hit Mr. Figlock, this baby was saved because once again the man happened to be in the right place at the right time. No baby ever fell on Mr. Figlock a third time, but it's probably just as well. He no doubt thought two falling baby coincidences were more than enough.

Another coincidence involving bouncing babies turned up in an ESP magazine named *Psychic*. The article described how a woman from New

York City flew out to see a cousin of hers in Denver, Colorado. During the visit her cousin told her about an amazing thing that happened in his building earlier in the afternoon. A small baby climbed up on a windowsill in an apartment on the eighth floor of the building and fell out. The infant tumbled eight stories without a scratch on him. The reason: instead of hitting the hard ground, he landed in some tall, soft shrubs near the building.

The incident was still on the woman's mind when she returned to her own apartment building in New York. What made it even more memorable was another story told to her by a neighbor. Just a few days before a small child fell out of an eighth floor apartment window in her building. Incredibly the baby's only injury was a bruised lip. Just before he hit the pavement the child landed on a window awning which broke his fall.

But that was not the part of the story that intrigued the woman. The baby fell at the exact time her cousin had been telling her the amazing story of the first falling baby in Denver.

Life is full of coincidences in which bad luck changes at just the right moment. For no particular reason just the right amount of good luck often pops up when people least expect it. It's as though some other force is at work helping us along, protecting us from what looks like certain disaster.

Neither disaster nor coincidence was on Captain Glenn McDonald's mind on that foggy night of May 17, 1978. All he was thinking about was finding his way home. McDonald was a tugboat captain who operated in the waters off the coast of Florida. He was heading back to shore that night when a heavy fog rolled in, blocking his view of the shore and throwing him off course. He could tell he was somewhere near the Pensacola airport because of the noise of planes passing overhead, but that wasn't enough to help him find his way back home. Since the fog showed no sign of lifting, he had the feeling he'd be stuck out on the water for a while.

A few miles away, another captain, this one the pilot of National Airlines Flight 193, didn't have McDonald's problem. His special guidance instruments were leading him through the fog right to the airport. In fact, he felt lucky that night that the fog wasn't as thick as it often got. Since he knew he wasn't far from the airport, he started taking the plane down to get ready for his landing.

He had barely dropped the plane a few feet when it hit something, hard. Then it was thrown back in the air. The pilot couldn't figure out what was going on. They were still supposed to be hundreds of feet in the air. What could they possibly have smacked into?

The plane slammed down again and this time stopped for good. The crew looked out the window and couldn't believe what they were seeing. The plane was lying on its belly in the ocean.

Something had gone wrong. Instead of being high in the air as they thought, they actually were just skimming the surface of the ocean, and when they started to dive down for the landing they smashed into the water.

The plane was sinking fast. Passengers were frantically unbuckling their seat belts and were scrambling out the emergency doors. Once they got outside there was a new danger. Gallons of jet fuel had already started to leak out, coating the water around them with a slick of explosive gas. One small spark could turn the whole crash site into a sea of flames. They could all be burned alive.

The crew and passengers had no way of knowing it at the time, but they were over three miles from shore, too far for most of them to swim. To make matters worse no one knew what happened to them. They had simply disappeared off the airport's radar screens when they crashed. Airport officials weren't sure where the plane went down, and they knew that because of the fog it could take hours to find it and rescue the people.

Fortunately one person did know where Flight 193 was. That was Captain Glenn McDonald. While he was lost and groping his way through the fog, he heard a plane's engine. It sounded close. Very close. He turned his head and saw a mammoth jetliner swooping out of the fog heading straight for him, barely skimming the surface of the water. About 300 yards away the plane suddenly slammed into the water, bounced in the air like a giant skipping stone, and hit hard a second time. McDonald suddenly forgot about being lost, turned his boat around, and headed for the sinking plane.

The people splashing in the water heard the deep grumble of a tugboat engine and out of the fog appeared Captain McDonald with a large barge trailing behind his tugboat. Everyone climbed aboard the boat and barge, and before the evening was over all but three people, who had been killed in the crash itself, were saved.

"If that barge hadn't been there," said a patrol boat captain who got to the crash scene much later, "there's no telling how many would have drowned." When a reporter asked McDonald how it was he happened to be drifting around in that particular part of the coast just as the plane crashed, the tugboat captain said he couldn't think of any particular reason why — except to save the passengers of Flight 193.

You can find the nick of time coincidence in the past as well as in the present. One of the most famous involved a brave group of Mormon pioneers, some crickets, and a flock of seagulls. The event happened in the mid-1800's near the spot now known as Salt Lake City, Utah. In those days many people were suspicious of anyone who was a Mormon because it was so different from other religions commonly practiced. And the Mormons suffered for this. In parts of the East and the Midwest where the Mormons lived, non-Mormons often made life hard for them. They stole Mormon cattle, burned down their churches, and beat them up. Finally it got so bad that the Mormon leader, Brigham Young, decided maybe it was time they moved to a place where they could practice their religion in peace and quiet. In those days the West was still wild and open to anyone who had the courage to try to settle it; so the Mormons loaded everything they owned onto wagons, grouped together in huge wagon trains miles long, and headed West. Even a life where they'd be in danger of many things, maybe even starvation, looked better than staying where they were.

The Mormons were looking for their own promised land and they found it, not far from that salt lake in Utah that was to give their city its name. Once they got settled, they saw their biggest problem would be food. They had taken enough with them to make it through the first winter, but they would have to grow and harvest enough to make it through the other winters to come. When their first spring started they were careful to get their crops planted as early as possible. The weather cooperated and it looked like it was going to be a good harvest. They started to breathe a little more easily. They were sure they would have enough food for the winter. But their good luck was not going to last.

One day while they were out in their fields,

they saw a huge black cloud moving their way from the west. It was coming too fast to be a rain cloud and they were beginning to wonder what it was when they heard a humming sound, very faint at first. Then it got louder and louder until that was all anyone could hear. Then huge insects started dropping to earth, first in twos and threes, then in dozens, then in hundreds, and finally in thousands so that the ground was covered with a squirming, buzzing blanket of giant crickets, each one as large as a mouse. That cloud had been a horde of insects passing over. When they spotted the green, lush Mormon crops they all apparently decided it was time to eat.

It was as though a mammoth plant-eating monster was crawling its way cross the acres of crops, chewing up everything in sight and leaving acres of dust and dead twigs behind. The farmers grabbed whatever they could find — shovels, rakes, boards, burlap sacks — and ran out into the fields where they tried to beat the insects to death. That was hopeless. There were more than they could kill.

One farmer came up with another idea that seemed to work. He flooded the irrigation ditches around the fields. When the insects tried to get across, they drowned. After a while so many crickets died that the ditches were clogged with their bodies and the ones that were still alive began using the piles of bodies as a bridge across the water.

24

Thousands of crickets were killed but it didn't seem to matter. There were thousands more to take their place. The Mormons didn't know what to do. The situation looked hopeless. In a few more hours all their crops would be destroyed. They fell to their knees and began to pray.

When they finished, they looked up. Gathering in the west was another black cloud moving their way just as the first one had. More crickets, the farmers thought. They would probably finish off what the first horde left behind. The Mormons were convinced they were doomed. Their winter food supply would be wiped out for sure.

But it wasn't a cloud of crickets. As it got closer the people could tell they were birds: seagulls. They had come to eat the insects, not the crops. The birds dropped down among them and went on a killing rampage, devouring every cricket in sight. In what seemed like minutes, all the crickets had been killed. When they had eaten their fill, the seagulls, as if on some mysterious signal, all took off and flew away as suddenly as they arrived. Although the Mormons did lose some crops, they had enough left for the winter.

Why the birds chose that particular moment to fly by no one was ever able to say. In the 125 years or so that the Mormons have lived in that area, they never again saw the birds flock together as they did that day. Some people have called the incident of the birds a very lucky coincidence. The Mormons call it a miracle.

*   *   *

Not all the nick of time coincidences are matters of life or death. Some might appear as just an odd stroke of good luck, canceling out a run of bad luck. For example, Richard Bach, the author of the book *Jonathan Livingston Seagull,* had something strange happen to him that would have seemed impossible without a time machine.

Bach is someone who loves to fly whenever he gets the chance. He especially likes old-time airplanes, the kind with double wings and open cockpits that putt along at 60 or 70 miles an hour. One of his favorites was an old 1929 biplane that he had bought and fixed up so it could fly again. It took him years to buy or have made all the parts needed to get it back into shape. One day a friend of his asked if he could have a try at flying the old plane, and Bach, a little worried for the ancient aircraft, said yes.

So the two men climbed into the plane's two cockpits — Bach in the rear co-pilot's cockpit and his friend as pilot in the front — and they took off. The flight went smoothly at first, but after a while the engine began acting funny. The friend was getting worried and suggested that they land someplace and take a look at it. He had just finished saying this when the two of them spotted what looked like an old airfield through a break in the trees. They couldn't believe their good luck. Until then they thought they were out in the middle of nowhere, miles from the nearest airport.

26

The field was old and rough. The landing bounced both of them and the plane around hard before they were finally able to stop. A quick check of the engine showed that just a small adjustment was all that was needed to fix it, but as they were getting back in the plane, they found they had a new, worse problem. One of the struts that supported the wings had snapped in the rough landing. It would be too risky to try taking off with it in that kind of shape.

It looked like they were going to be staying at that old airfield a long time. They were miles from anywhere and, to make the matter worse, the part they needed just wasn't made anymore. In fact it probably hadn't been made in over 30 years.

As the two men stood there trying to figure out what to do, an old man wandered up to them and asked if he could help. Bach said jokingly he could if he had a 30-year-old wing strut for an antique airplane. The man studied the broken part for a moment and then turned to Bach and his friend. "Follow me," he said mysteriously.

He walked over to an old barn that wasn't more than 20 feet from where they were standing and unlocked the rusty old padlock on the door. When it swung open and the men's eyes got used to the darkness, they couldn't believe what they saw. The place was filled with old airplane parts, some even older than their plane. The man explained that in his younger days he used to do quite a bit of flying and owned several airplanes. As each broke down he saved what parts he could and stored them in this barn, which he owned. He just happened to be visiting the old airfield that day and saw Bach and his friend land in their old-time airplane.

The man rummaged through the jumble of odd parts and after a few minutes pulled out a wing strut. It looked like an exact copy of the one that had broken. Bach and his friend tried to fit it on the airplane; it was perfect. They couldn't believe their good luck. Instead of having to spend days there, they only needed a couple of hours to make the repairs and take off.

As he was flying away from the airfield, Bach was thinking how odd it was that they just happened to drop down on that particular out-of-the-way airfield on the very day that the only person who owned that barn full of parts just happened to be visiting. Just as odd, thought Bach, was the fact that the man had exactly the part they needed, in spite of the fact that no one had been making it for over 30 years, and furthermore that the plane had rolled to a stop not more than 20 feet from where that part was stored. Very strange.

What can be equally strange is a coincidence that some experts have called the "library angel." It works this way. You're looking for a particular book or piece of paper, and you walk into a library or a room full of files not knowing where to begin. According to the library angel coincidence, what you should do is not to start looking in any systematic way, but just wander around and just pick up the first item that appeals to you. If the library angel is with you, that will be the item you want.

One of the most famous cases of this involved an Egyptologist named Thomas Young who had been trying to figure out how to read hieroglyphics, the strange picture writings of the ancient Egyptians. The year was 1822. No one had yet managed to read the writing that was on the Egyptian tombs, monuments, and the ancient scrolls of papyrus that archaeologists had dug up. Thomas himself had spent years on the problem with no luck.

One particular morning he was puzzling over a piece of Egyptian papyrus. He still had no luck figuring it out, but he could read three names on it: Apollonius, Antigonus, and Antimachus. That was only because they were printed in Greek letters and not hieroglyphics. Everything else was a total mystery.

After a few hours he gave up and moved on to some other work. Just that morning a piece of ancient Greek scroll had arrived in the mail and he decided to take a look at it. As he glanced over it quickly, he thought it wasn't very intertesting, just old. He was about to put it aside when out of the corner of his eye he noticed the scroll mentioned three very familiar names: Apollonius, Antigonus, and Antimachus.

It didn't seem possible but it was true. He had

in his hands a Greek translation of the Egyptian papyrus he had been reading minutes before. This was the key he needed to break the language code. As he sat there he thought how tremendously lucky it was that this ancient Greek scroll had not only survived in one piece after more than two thousand years, but had somehow made its way thousands of miles to his particular house in England, and happened to arrive on the very morning he was reading the Egyptian version of the same document. The odds against that happening had to be a million to one. Just the same, here it was, courtesy of the powers of coincidence.

3

Meetings of Coincidence

A family reunion was the last thing on Hercule Pinon's mind as he boarded the London-bound ferry that chilly, foggy morning in Le Havre, France. Pinon was a spy, working against his own country in behalf of the Germans. The year was 1916, and Pinon knew that it was just a matter of months before Germany and France would be at war with each other. Before that happened he had received orders to make one last appointment with his spy contact to get further orders. A meeting in London, he was told, was safer than anywhere in France, where he might be suspected.

What Pinon didn't know was that his days as a spy were over. The French government had discovered who he was and, with the cooperation of the British police, planned to have him arrested as soon as he landed on English soil. By arranging to have Pinon arrested out of the country, French intelligence figured that they would keep his fellow spies from ever finding out what happened to him. It would seem as though Mr. Pinon simply disappeared off the face of the earth.

Everything went as planned. Pinon walked off the boat and handed his passport over to the customs agent. When the man saw who he was, he gave a secret signal and two plainclothed policemen grabbed Pinon and escorted him away to an interrogation room. After the commotion of the arrest was over, the customs man went back to his desk and looked at the next passport. It belonged to Mrs. Hercule Pinon, the French spy's wife. The British police were a little confused. They hadn't received any orders to arrest Mrs. Pinon but, they figured, just to be on the safe side they'd better grab her too.

Pinon realized when he was beaten and admitted to the police that he was a spy. He answered all their questions but seemed a little confused when they told him they had also arrested his wife. "But I have no wife," he kept insisting. This made the police suspicious that maybe he was trying to protect her. They went to the other room where she was being held and started grilling her about her husband's espionage work. She seemed just as confused as Mr. Pinon. "But I have no husband!" she kept saying. After asking more questions, the police started to believe that both the man and woman were telling the truth. Now the police were getting confused.

To clear everything up once and for all, they decided to bring the man and woman face to face. When they did, the mystery was solved. The man and the woman had been husband and wife 24 years ago. At that time they decided to separate, they thought, forever. So in all those 24 years they never got divorced and had never seen each other — until today. As it turned out both had by chance taken the same ferry, and — even more coincidentally — lined up at the customs desk so that Mr. Pinon happened to stand in front of Mrs. Pinon. Because of the years apart neither recognized the other. In the end it turned out to be a brief but memorable reunion. Mrs. Pinon was cleared of any suspicion of spying and was released. Mr. Pinon was arrested and sent to France for imprisonment.

In every history of coincidental meetings you come across a fair share of cases in which some of the most unlikely people meet each other again in the most unlikely circumstances. For some reason many of these seem to happen to husband and wives or ex-husbands and ex-wives. For example, a few years ago an Englishman named Walter Davis was divorced from his wife and a few months later felt he'd like to get married again. He decided to find his second wife the modern way: through a marriage bureau that used a computer to match men and women. The bureau had him fill out a special form describing himself and send it in. At the marriage bureau the information was fed into a computer that matched him with someone who would make the most suitable wife.

A few weeks after he sent in his questionnaire, Davis got his answer in the mail. Nervously he opened the envelope to see who his new bride would be. When he read the name he couldn't believe it. It was his ex-wife. She had applied at the same marriage bureau and, in spite of the divorce, the computer thought that she and her ex-husband made a perfect match. Figuring that the computer knew more than they did about marriage, the ex-Mr. and Mrs. Davis got married to each other again.

Other coincidental meetings can have strange endings, such as the one mentioned in the book *Remarkable Occurrences* by author John Train. He writes that in the city of Prague, Czechoslovakia, there was a woman named Vera Czermak who found out her husband was planning to run away from home. She was so upset she decided to commit suicide by jumping out of a third floor window in her house.

She jumped, but she was lucky. As she was falling a man happened to be walking by the building and she landed right on top of him. He broke her fall and saved her life. The man did not make out quite so well. He was killed by the impact of the falling woman. He was also Mr. Czermak, the woman's husband.

Fortunately not all meetings of coincidence end up so disastrously. One that was especially happy took place in a small town in New York State about 25 years ago. The story, as told in *Reader's*

Digest magazine, began early one Christmas Eve day in an old, rundown church. The young pastor and his wife woke up that morning to find that a wild rainstorm during the night had soaked through one wall of the church and a huge hunk of plaster had fallen away. The result was a big, ugly hole right behind the altar. There was no time to get it fixed, and even if he had the time, the pastor didn't have the money. The parish was poor.

Later that same day the pastor was at a charity auction when one of the items put up for bidding was an enormous, handmade gold-and-ivory-colored tablecloth. No one was really interested in it except for the pastor who bought it for about six dollars. The huge cloth, he explained to his wife, could go up behind the altar to hide the hole in the church wall.

That same afternoon the pastor was unlocking the church to hang the cloth when he noticed a lone woman shivering in the cold by a bus stop. Since the bus wasn't due to come for another half hour, he invited her into the church to get warm.

The woman slipped into a pew, first rubbing her hands together to warm them, and then kneeling briefly to say a prayer. When she looked up, the minister was busy hanging up the tablecloth. It turned out to be a perfect cover for the hole. He was about to tell her the story of how he got it, since she seemed so interested, when she started telling him a stranger story. She said that years before when she was living in Vienna, Austria, she had a tablecloth that looked exactly like this one. It was a gift from her husband. He had her initials put on it. When World War II broke out, she was separated from her husband and never saw him again. She later heard that he died in a prison camp.

Taking a closer look she realized that it was her tablecloth. There in one corner were her initials just as she described them. The minister offered to give it back to her but she turned him down. She didn't need it anymore, she said. What she really needed was work. She had just come to town that day to apply for a job as a governess with a local family but was turned down. Now she was heading back to her small apartment in the city where she lived. She thanked him for his offer and when the bus came, she climbed on and went home.

The same night after Christmas Eve services, many people complimented the minister on the new hanging. One man in particular stopped to talk. He was an old man, the local watchmaker, who had lived in town for years. He too said he liked the cloth and mentioned how it reminded him of an elaborate tablecloth he had bought his wife years ago when he had a large house in Vienna.

When he heard this, the minister thought the man might also like to hear the story of the woman from the bus stop who was in the church earlier that day. The old man was tremendously excited. Together he and the minister located the family that had interviewed his wife earlier that day and got her city address from them. The next day, Christmas, the man joined his wife from whom he'd been separated since Warld War II!

As coincidences go there are few that are this complicated. Because the rainstorm just happened to wipe out a huge hunk of the wall; because the minister just happened to find that particular tablecloth to cover the hold; because he just happened to meet the woman who owned it, who also just happened to be visiting that town that one day *and* happened to be standing by that particular bus stop; and because the woman's husband not only just happened to live in the same town but happened to worship at that same church, two people who had given each other up for dead were reunited.

Most coincidences in which two long-lost people meet each other are a little simpler but can be just as amazing. For example, as a boy, James Parrish III always dreamed of seeing his father again. The boy lived with his mother in Portland, Oregon, but the father had moved to Fort Worth, Texas, when James was seven years old. And that was the last time they had seen each other.

Young James had always wanted to save up his money and travel down to Fort Worth as a surprise to his father. Finally one summer, when he was 19 years old, he had enough money to do it.

He bought a bus ticket to Texas and sat restlessly through the long 54 hours it took to get there. He knew when he arrived at Fort Worth he would have another problem: identifying his father. It had been over 12 years since he had last seen him and he wasn't even sure he'd recognize him. All he knew was that his father was a car dealer.

Eventually he got to Fort Worth but was so low on money he decided to hitchhike. He stuck out his thumb and in a few minutes a car pulled over. There was an older man at the wheel. The young Parrish asked the man if he knew where James Parrish's car showroom was. The man said he knew it very well. He was James Parrish. The very first car that stopped to pick up young James that morning just happened to be driven by his father whom he'd been waiting to see for over a decade.

What makes some coincidences more interesting than others is not how they happen but the fact that they can happen more than once, as they did to the 19th-century French poet, Emile Deschamps. All of his coincidences revolved around a plum pudding.

It started when he was a boy in a boarding school in France. One of his schoolmates, a boy named Fortgibu, had gone to England on one school vacation and brought back a special English treat, plum pudding. He gave some to Deschamps who had never had it before. Although he didn't think English food was worth touching with a 10-foot fork, Deschamps had to admit the pudding was good.

Ten years later, Deschamps was ambling through a side street in Paris and passed a restaurant where a friend of his worked. He decided to drop in and pay a surprise visit. While in the kitchen talking to his friend, he noticed that the chef was making plum pudding. That reminded him of the one he had so long ago and he asked the chef if he could have a piece.

The chef explained that it wasn't his to offer. He said he was preparing it as a special order for one of the restaurant's customers. Perhaps if Deschamps asked the man who placed the order he could get a piece from him.

When Deschamps went out to see who it was, he was pleased to discover that it was none other than his old classmate, Mr. Fortgibu, whom he hadn't seen since school. They made a little joke about meeting over the same dish and then sat down and ate it.

Years later Deschamps was at a dinner party and noticed plum pudding was one of the dishes being served. This reminded him of his meeting with Fortgibu, so he told the story of how the two of them only seemed to meet when there was a plum pudding around. In fact the last time he had eaten the dish was that time he ran into Fortgibu in the restaurant. Someone at the table joked that since the plum pudding was there already, Fortgibu could not be far behind.

The evening went on with no Fortgibu in sight

(no one really expected him to appear anyway) and the talk moved on from discussing Deschamps' plum pudding coincidence to other matters. The meal was almost over and dessert was about to be served when there was a knock at the door. It was someone who was invited to a party in another apartment in the same building, but had lost his way. Deschamps turned to see who it was and saw his plum pudding friend, Fortgibu. "My hair stood on end," Deschamps said later.

Slightly more mysterious was the coincidence of the man who met himself, or seemed to meet himself, in a strange city. The man was a Mr. George D. Bryson who was traveling through Kentucky, and on the spur of the moment decided to get off the train at Louisville. He had never visited the city before but always wanted to. He asked around and was recommended the Brown hotel as one of the best places to stay. He checked in and was assigned his room, 307. Just before he went upstairs, he decided to play a small joke on the woman working at the mail desk. He walked over and asked if there was any mail for a Mr. Bryson.

She turned around and checked and, to his total surprise, handed him a letter. He looked at the envelope. It was addressed to a Mr. George D. Bryson, Room 307. He was totally mystified. No one, including himself, knew that he was going to stop at Louisville much less stay at this particular hotel and in room 307. When he opened the letter the mystery cleared up. It was addressed to another George Bryson who not only had the same name right down to the middle initial but even had stayed in that same room. The other Mr. Bryson as it happened had just checked out from room 307 earlier that day.

The following story, told by author Max Gunther in his book *The Luck Factor*, begins with a French scientist named Alphonse Bertillon who came up with what looked like a foolproof way of identifying people. For a long time the police couldn't be sure about the criminals they caught. Positively identifying a person is not as easy as it seems. Many people look alike and crooks can easily change their appearances by shaving off or growing beards and moustaches or by using a dozen other different tricks. Bertillon found one thing that could not be changed or disguised: a certain set of body measurements.

In 1870 he announced what he called the Bertillon System. He claimed that no two people had the same measurements for things like the size of their skulls and the length of certain bones in their bodies. He even had a special formula that made it simple to use his system of measurements. He tested his method on thousands of people and found, as he predicted, that everyone's measurements were totally different. It wasn't long before police departments saw the Bertillon System was the best method of making positive identifications. After 1870 when police arrested a criminal, they measured his body with the Bertillon System and recorded the numbers on his record.

That all changed one day in 1903, when a man named Will West was being admitted to Leavenworth Penitentiary in Kansas. The warden asked West if he had ever been arrested before. (People who had committed other crimes were given tougher treatment in prison in those days.) West said he hadn't, but somehow the warden didn't believe him. There was something very familiar about West. On a hunch, he had his guards take Bertillon measurements of West and check them against prison files.

Sure enough the files turned up a William West who had been tried, convicted, and imprisoned for murder. The warden had his proof. Not only did the convict have the same name but he had the exact same body measurements. No two people in the world could have the same Bertillon numbers, the warden said. It was impossible.

But West kept insisting it was possible and made such a row about never having been in prison before that the prison officials doublechecked their records. There was a convicted murderer named William West, but the weird thing was he was *still* there in prison and had been for years. He had been in prison so long, he was almost completely forgotten by prison authorities.

When the warden had the other West brought to his office he got the surprise of his life. Not only did the two Will Wests have the same name and same Bertillon numbers, they looked identical enough to be twin brothers, even though they were not related.

It happened at that time that one of the crime experts working at the prison was trying out a new system of identification, taking fingerprints instead of body measurements. He claimed it was simpler and really more foolproof than Bertillon's System. This case of the two Will Wests, he said, would be the perfect chance to find out if it worked.

He took both men's fingerprints and compared. They were completely different from one another. As a result of the Will West coincidence it wasn't long before other prison officials and police departments around the country stopped using the bone measurements of Mr. Bertillon and turned to the system of positive identification still used today: fingerprinting.

Of all the stories of coincidental meetings of two strangers there is none that can top the bizarre story about the king and the innkeeper. The whole thing happened in Italy in 1900 in the month of July. The man who was then king of Italy, Umberto I, had traveled to the small town of Monza where he was to hand out awards to the winners of a big athletic event that was going to be held. The king arrived the night before the event and stayed at a small local inn.

That evening the king sat down to dine and the

owner of the inn took charge of serving him. Umberto immediately noticed that the man looked exactly like him and mentioned this. As the two men talked he found out that they had much more in common than just their looks. First of all the man had the same first name as the king. He not only had been born in the same city as the king but he was born on the same day too. Umberto also found out that both he and the innkeeper were married on the same day to women with the same first name, Margherita. Umberto later had a child, a boy whom he called Vittorio. So did the innkeeper. Lastly, the day Umberto was crowned king, the innkeeper opened his inn.

With all these coincidences the king said he was amazed they had never seen each other before. The innkeeper said actually they had, twice. The man had served in the army and had twice gotten medals for bravery, once in 1870 and again in 1876, on the very days the king received similar decorations.

The king was so impressed by how closely this man's life copied his own, he decided to give him a special award at the games the next day. He instructed one of his generals to tell the man to be there so he could receive the honor.

The following day when the time came for presenting the award, the innkeeper didn't appear. Umberto sent one of his aides to look for him. A short time later a messenger came back with sad news. The innkeeper had been shot in a hunting accident that morning and died. When he heard this Umberto replied, "Find out when the funeral takes place. I wish to attend."

He had just finished saying this when a man with a wild look on his face pushed his way through the crowd. He pulled out a pistol and fired at Umberto three times. The first shot missed but the next two hit the king and killed him almost instantly. He was buried the same day as his exact double. Officially, history says that King Umberto I of Italy was killed by an assassin, but if you want to be more precise about the facts, you would have to say that he was actually the victim of a truly strange and deadly coincidence.

4

Finders Keepers

You probably already know that there are two kinds of missing things: those that get lost forever, and those that seem to hide for a while and then reappear when you least expect them. And what usually brings them back is a good coincidence. Like the ones in the story of Edward Sothern's gold matchbox.

During the late 1800's Edward Sothern was a popular stage actor in England. He had several rich and impressive friends of whom the richest and most impressive was the son of Queen Victoria, the Prince of Wales. Sothern and the prince enjoyed doing many things together, especially horseback riding on fox hunts. One day the prince gave Sothern a small gold matchbox as a token of his friendship. Honored by the gift, Sothern wore the small gold box as a decoration on his watch chain.

He wore his watch and chain all the time, even while riding, a habit that turned out to be costly.

One day during a hunt Sothern's horse threw him. When he got up he realized that in the fall his gold matchbox had broken free. A number of people helped him search for it in the surrounding shrubs and grass but no one was able to find it. Sothern by then was very attached to the small gold box, so he had a jeweler make another one, an exact copy of the first, as a replacement.

He had better luck hanging onto that one and years after he made a gift of it to Sam Sothern, one of his two sons, both of whom had followed their father's footsteps and become actors themselves. Sam was about to leave on a tour of Australia and his father gave him the small gold charm as a going away gift. Sam later gave the same gold box to a close friend of his, a fellow actor named Mr. Labertouche.

Sam didn't give much thought to that box or the original from which it was copied until about 20 years later, when he was out horseback riding in England, a sport passed on to him by his father. He stopped to talk to a local farmer and during the conversation happened to mention his name. Hearing it the farmer asked, "Are you Edward Sothern's son?" When Sam said he was, the farmer asked him to come to his house. He said he had something special to show Sam.

That something special turned out to be a small gold matchbox, not the copy Sam had gotten from his father, but the original one that had been the gift of the Prince of Wales. The farmer said he had just uncovered it that morning in his fields and noticed the inscription on it.

Sam was as impressed by the farmer's honesty as by the lucky coincidence of happening to be around on the exact day the box was discovered. It was such a good story that he mentioned it in the next letter he wrote to his brother Edward, who at that time was traveling through the United States with a theatrical troupe.

The letter eventually caught up with the brother while he was on a train traveling to his next tour stop. At the time he was reading it, he was sitting next to a young actor who had just joined the troupe that morning. He told the man the story of Sam finding the gold matchbox, describing the original and added that his father had a copy made when he lost the first one. At that point Edward wondered aloud about what had happened to the copy Sam eventually gave away.

"Here it is," the new actor said, pulling out his watch chain. He explained that a few years ago he had been given the small gold box as a gift from a Mr. Labertouche, the same person Sam had given his matchbox to so many years before. Everyone involved in the matchbox discoveries had to admit it was a dazzling set of coincidences: that Sam not only happened to be around on the very day the first one was uncovered, but that his brother just happened to be sitting next to the man who owned the second one while reading Sam's letter describing his lucky find.

A much less complicated lost and found story involves a very special gift an Englishman named Ahern Benham gave his wife. Benham had found a rare antique ring that had a bizarre distinction to it. Sealed up inside was a lock of hair from the head of the Duke of Wellington, one of the great military heroes of British history. Benham presented it to his wife as a wedding gift. In time, it became one of her favorite rings.

One evening while she was at a party, she discovered the ring had slipped off her finger. In spite of a thorough search of the room, no one could find any trace of it. That was the last she saw or heard of the ring until 18 years later when she got a letter from a sister who was living in Australia.

The sister mentioned how an unusual discovery had helped raise money for a local church. She said she had asked a friend in London to buy a pair of gloves and send them to her. The day they arrived she took them out of the box and eagerly tried them on. One didn't fit well because something was stuck in one of the fingers. When she shook it out she found a beautiful antique ring. Inside was an inscription saying there was a lock of hair from the Duke of Wellington sealed in it.

At that time the church was having an auction to raise money, so she donated it to the minister as one item they could offer. A local man bought the rare ring for a few thousand dollars. When Mrs. Benham read this she tracked down the man, explained the history of it to him, and was able to buy it back.

Sometimes, as in the case of the gold matchbox, lost items have a way of finding their way back to their owners without any help. This happened to a Mrs. Elsie Kleiner who was on vacation with her young son in the town of Strassburg, Germany, one day in 1914. She brought her camera with her and took a few snapshots of her son and dropped them off at a local store to be developed. Soon after, fighting with France broke out near there and she had to leave the city without picking up her film.

Two years later she was vacationing in the city of Frankfurt, this time with her daughter. She bought a roll of film for her camera and later dropped it off to be developed. This time she made it back to get her pictures. When she saw the photos she was furious. Somehow the store had sold her a used not a new roll of film. As a result every one of her snapshots was a double exposure. The big surprise came when she took a closer look at one of the double exposures. She could barely make out in the background a picture of her son. Somehow that same roll of film she used in Strassburg two years before found its way to Frankfurt and back into her hands.

Even non-lost items somehow seem to get back to where they belong. A woman named Anne Parrish from Colorado Springs, Colorado, was visiting Paris for the first time in her life and was spending much of her time just walking around the city taking in the sights. One day she and her husband came across an outdoor bookstore that sold used books. While poking through a pile of children's books she found a copy of *Jack Frost and Other Stories.*

She picked it up and showed it to her husband saying, "Look at this. I was brought up on this in my nursery days and I haven't seen a copy since." She had barely finished speaking when she opened the book and found written inside her own name and childhood address in Colorado Springs. Her book had preceded her to Paris and waited there for her.

Probably the eeriest story of the book that refused to stay lost was the *Divine Comedy* written by the great Italian poet, Dante Alighieri. Shortly after his death in 1321, Dante's two sons, Jacopo and Pietro, realized that only part of their father's masterpiece was with his papers. They knew he had finished the work but couldn't find the rest of the book. Eventually they gave up the search thinking that maybe he had destroyed or lost the rest.

A short time later Jacopo had a dream in which his father appeared to him wearing glowing white robes. Jacopo asked the vision of his father if the *Divine Comedy* had been finished. The ghostly figure nodded yes. Jacopo then asked where the rest of it was. The figure in white led him to a room in the house that had already been searched. He went over to one wall, pointed to a spot on it and disappeared.

Although Jacopo didn't believe much in dreams, the next day he thought it wouldn't hurt to take a look where he saw the finger point. When he entered the room he found a small set of venetian blinds hanging on that spot on the wall. He lifted them up and found behind them a small window.

On the sill was a pile of papers, covered with dust and half rotted with mold. Brushing away the dirt he could see his father's writing. The vision, or whatever it was, was right. This completed the missing part of Dante's masterpiece. Why the son happened to dream about that room, a room he and his brother had already searched, is a question no one has ever answered. Maybe it was luck. Maybe.

Just as lucky and just as peculiar was a message in a bottle that washed up on the beach outside of a small Japanese fishing village one day in 1935. It was a large bottle' with a piece of wood poked inside. The message had been scratched onto the wood by a sailor named Chunosuke Matsuyama. It told the story of how his ship was wrecked.

A storm had driven the vessel onto a coral reef in the Pacific Ocean, and the crew couldn't free her. They also couldn't leave the ship because it carried no lifeboats and the nearest land was too far away for anyone to reach by swimming. The best the crew of 44 could do was sit and wait in the hopes that another ship would pass by and rescue them.

At the time Matsuyama carved his message, things didn't look too promising. Their food supply was almost gone, and no ship had been spotted for days. So the world would know what happened, just in case the crew didn't survive, Matsuyama wrote down their story and set it drifting along ocean currents inside a bottle.

That was back in 1784. For over 150 years the bottle slowly moved along carried by waves, completely unnoticed until finally its trip ended on the shores of that small Japanese village. What made the bottle's choice of a landing spot so uncanny was that it was the same village where Chunosuke Matsuyama was born more than a century before. His message had come home.

Sometimes even the smallest coincidence can make a big difference in solving a mystery, as in the strange case of one of the stingiest counterfeiters in the history of U.S. crime. He was an elusive crook whom the Secret Service had been stalking for years. They nicknamed him "Old Eight-Eighty" after the file number, 880, that had been assigned to his case. In one way Old Eight-Eighty seemed to be a master criminal. For nine years he managed to avoid capture by the Secret Service, the government agency in charge of catching counterfeiters. Thousands of warnings had been sent out about him to stores all over New York City where Old Eight-Eighty operated, but no one ever seemed to notice his counterfeit bills.

It's not that he was a good counterfeiter. He was one of the worst the Secret Service had ever seen. He used cheap paper that felt nothing like real money. The one-dollar bills, which were his specialty, were sloppy. The portrait of George Washington on the bill was dark and smudgy. He used the same serial number over and over again and in one batch of bills he even got the name of the first president wrong, spelling it "Wahsington."

He was hard to catch because he was so stingy with his phony money. While big-time counterfeiters sometimes handed out hundreds of thousands of dollars in fake ten- and twenty-dollar bills in a year, Old Eight-Eighty handed out no more than two or three phony dollars a day, seldom totaling more than five or six hundred dollars the whole year. And because he specialized only in one-dollar bills, which few people look at that closely, his sloppy work was hardly ever spotted.

The Secret Service got their first big break in the case because of two boys who just happened to be walking by a vacant lot in Manhattan one day in 1948. They were poking through some rubbish thrown out of a burning building by firemen when they found a small pile of phony money, all one-dollar bills. It was so fake looking they thought that maybe it was stage money and took a couple handfuls home to play with.

One of the boys' fathers saw the fake cash and called the police who called in the Secret Service. As soon as they saw the sloppy bills, the Secret Service agents knew they were hot on the trail of the elusive Eight-Eighty. They went to the building where the fire was and found in one of the old, run-down apartments a 73-year-old man named Edward Mueller. In his small room was a little printing press and a pile of familiar looking one-dollar bills. They caught their man.

Mueller was a widower who lived alone and spent his days roaming the streets collecting junk in a small pushcart. He had no relatives or friends to take care of him so he decided to take care of himself. He picked up what money he could doing odd jobs and when he ran low on cash, he just printed some more.

He wasn't too greedy with his counterfeiting. He never printed anything bigger than one-dollar bills and never gave his fake bills to the same person more than once so no one ever lost more than a dollar in dealing with him.

If there hadn't been a fire in his building, if firemen hadn't thrown out some of his junk, and if those boys hadn't come across the fake bills the day after the fire, the case of file 880 might have remained unsolved. Some thought the punishment later doled out to him by the court was a little harsh: he had to spend a few weeks in jail and pay the federal court a fine of one *genuine* dollar.

It can be as difficult to find a whole group of people as it was to find Old Eight-Eighty, as was the case in one of the great historical mysteries, the Lost Colony of Sir Walter Raleigh. One lucky coincidence has lead many historians to believe that they've found the lost colony. But before we get to that you should know a little about the colony before it got lost.

The famous Sir Walter Raleigh was given some land in North America, and in 1587 a group of English men and women led by Governor John White sailed over from England and settled on Roanoke Island off the coast of North Carolina. They were all adventurous families with names like Cooper, Dare, and Sampson, who had come over to try a new life on a new land.

Life was hard for these pioneers their first year. They survived it but got dangerously low on items such as gunpowder and tools. If the colony was going to continue, White decided they needed more supplies. To get them, he gathered up a crew and prepared to sail back to England. Just before he left, he told those that stayed behind that if they had to move the settlement to a different area, to leave behind some sign for him so he knew where to find them. Then he left.

White wasn't able to return to North America for two years. Pirates and war made the trip across the Atlantic too treacherous. Finally things calmed down enough for White to make a quick return trip to his colony. When he got to where his settlement had been, he found it was completely deserted, a ghost town. There was no clue of where everyone went or why they left. Since he could find no bodies he assumed everyone got out in one piece. The only thing that might have indicated where the vanished settlers went was one word, *Croatoan*, scratched into the side of a post.

Croatoan, White knew, was the name of an island to the south of Roanoke Island where a tribe known as the Hatteras Indians lived. He wanted to go there and search for the missing settlers but he didn't have enough time or enough supplies to make such a long extra trip. Sadly, he climbed back on his ship and headed back to England. From that day on what happened to that group of settlers has remained a mystery.

Just recently historians started piecing together some interesting bits of information about a tribe called the Lumbee Indians who still live in the Lumber River Valley in North Carolina. For Indians they are strange looking. Many have light skin and blue eyes. A few even have blond hair. There are records going back to the 1880's that tell of travelers meeting light-skinned Indians like the Lumbees who spoke a strange kind of English and who also claimed to have ancestors who could read English.

Now historians know that the Hatteras Indians

moved from Croatoan Island about 60 years after the Roanoke settlers disappeared. They settled in the Lumber River Valley where the Lumbee Indians are today. It's a good possibility that many of these same Lumbee Indians are descendants of those Hatteras Indians and White's settlers. What makes it almost certain is a strange coincidence that links the Indians with the lost colony. Many of the Indians have family names like Cooper, Dare, and Sampson, the same names as those who first came over with Governor White.

5

Strange Animal Coincidences

Animals, as we all know, are dumb. Or are they? Every so often you hear a story that makes you think twice about how much animals know and how much they can do. You can explain the story any way you want by saying the animals were lucky, they were super-smart, or just took advantage of certain coincidences. The fact remains that some of the stories are extraordinary.

Like the one about little John Murphy's pet pigeon. John Murphy was a 12-year-old boy who was living in a small West Virginia town in 1940. One night he had a horrible pain in his side. His parents called the doctor who said it sounded like appendicitis. The boy would have to be taken to the hospital and operated on.

The nearest hospital was over 100 miles away. The parents carried John to the car and rushed him to the emergency room where the surgery team was waiting for him. In a short amount of time the appendix was out, and John was out of danger. All that was needed, the doctors said, was for him to spend a few more days in the hospital to recover.

While he was resting John missed his parents, and he also missed his pet pigeon. He hoped his bird was being fed and wasn't wondering where its owner was. These questions were answered one night when John heard what sounded like someone rapping on his window. He didn't know who it could be. After all he was on the fourth floor, a little too high up for anyone to reach. He could barely see out the window. The sky was pitch black and there was a blinding snowstorm going on outside. He called in the nurse who looked outside and saw a very cold-looking pigeon staring in at her. It seemed to be trying to get into the room. When the boy saw it, he said it reminded him of his pet and asked the nurse to let it in to get warm. When she opened the window it flew over near the boy's bed and sat on the floor. That's when he was certain it was his.

The nurse at first thought he was making up the story so he could have an excuse to keep the bird, but he said he could prove that it was his. His bird had a small metal band around one ankle with the number 169 stamped on it. The nurse looked and found the band and the number, 169. The hospital staff was so impressed with the bird's faithfulness to the boy that they let it stay in a small box by the bed while the boy was recovering.

No one could figure out how the bird managed to get there. The parents said the bird couldn't have followed their car because it was still at home when they got back from bringing their son to the hospital. It didn't seem possible that this bird could manage to fly over 100 miles through a blinding snowstorm to a strange city and not only locate the building but even the room where its master was sleeping. It didn't seem possible, everyone said; but that still didn't change the fact that the bird actually did it.

Of course, other animals have pulled off equally spectacular stunts. One famous case had to do with a Persian cat named Sugar. One day the family that owned Sugar had to move from their house in San Diego, California, to their new place in Oklahoma, thousands of miles away. They planned to take Sugar with them, but Sugar had other plans.

Sugar was willing to go but not by car. She hated riding in cars. Nevertheless the family grabbed her and everyone piled into the car getting ready to make the 1,500-mile trip to their new home. The car had barely gone a mile when Sugar broke free and jumped out an open window. The family tried to get her, but she was too fast for them. Everyone looked for the cat but no one had any luck. After a while they all had to pile back in the car and leave Sugar behind.

A year passed and the family was sitting around the kitchen table one night when a cat jumped in the open window. They could tell right away it was Sugar from a slight hip deformity that gave her a peculiar walk. Everyone was happy to see her but they all had a hard time believing it was Sugar. In order to get to their house, she had to cross over the Rocky Mountains and walk part of the 1,500 miles over a blazing desert. How she managed to track them down to a strange house in a strange state no one could even guess. One thing was obvious, Sugar would do anything to avoid riding in a car.

It's hard to top a story like Sugar's, but according to the *Book of Lists*, there was another cat named Daisy who managed to perform a homing feat that was at least as dazzling. Daisy's life with one family began when they were vacationing in a small town in upper New York State one summer. The family did what was a pretty cruel thing. They adopted Daisy for the summer but, once vacation was over, they left her behind and went back to New York City. Most summer pets abandoned this way try to get by as best they can through the winter and many die when left on their own.

Daisy was no ordinary pet. She had a comfortable life with her summer family and wasn't about to give it up that easily. As a result, one morning the family was walking out the front door of their building in the middle of New York City and found Daisy sitting on their front steps. She was holding a kitten in her mouth. She had not only managed to trek the hundreds of miles from the summer home and find her adopted family out of the millions of people who live in New York City, but she also managed to bring her kitten along as well.

That alone was enough to impress them. But there was more to come. After resting a few days Daisy disappeared, leaving her kitten behind. A few weeks later she turned up a second time, carrying a second kitten. She dropped this one off, rested up, and went back for a third one. Then she did the same thing all over again with a fourth kitten and again with a fifth, her last. Only after all five of the members of her own cat family were together did she stop and settle down once and for all in her new home.

How do animals do this? Is it pure luck or can animals somehow sense where to go? One animal expert, Dr. Bastian Schmidt, tried to find out by taking three dogs, one at a time, to a strange part of the countryside and releasing them to see how well they found their way home. Two dog watchers followed each animal to see how each would do. Schmidt found that some animals were better at finding their way home from an unknown place than others. One dog got hopelessly lost while the other two, after a little wandering around, managed to head off in the direction for home.

Animals seem to have a homing sense, but it is hard to tell how good it is from experiments like these. First of all the dogs were heading back to a home they knew, not one they had never seen before. Secondly, they only had to travel a distance of a dozen miles, not the hundreds of miles covered by super-pets like Sugar and Daisy. It is still hard, if not impossible, to understand how any kind of sense of direction or ability to track someone could work over distances that long.

Equally strange are things some dogs have done, showing they seemed to have some kind of sixth sense about danger. The first story of this kind was told by a man named A.A. Smith who was a sailor and had a pet dog named Harold that used to be there waiting on the docks when his ship came in. Since the ships followed a fairly predictable schedule there was nothing all that amazing about the dog showing up. But once Smith was injured, badly burned in an engine room accident while at sea, and had to be taken to a hospital on shore for treatment. No one knew he was coming and he didn't even come into shore on his regular ship.

Just the same, as they took him off the ship and were putting him in an ambulance, there sitting on the dock was his dog, Harold. He followed the ambulance all the way to the hospital and patiently sat down by the front door of the building. He refused to leave and ate very little food as he waited for his master.

Smith had been told about his pet waiting outside and was as puzzled as everyone else about how his dog just seemed to know when he was taken to shore. To test his dog's special intuition, Smith decided to play a trick the day he was released. He planned to go out the back door of the hospital, then go around the front and surprise Harold.

But when the time came to leave he had barely opened the back door when he heard a familiar bark. Sitting there a few feet away was Harold. "I have often wondered," Smith later said, "how did Harold know?"

Another dog who became famous for his nose for trouble was a St. Bernard named Barry. He was a mascot of the monks of the Hospice of St. Bernard who specialized in rescuing stranded travelers in the Swiss Alps during the treacherous winter months. In the 14 years Barry lived during the early 1800's he saved the lives of over 40 people. Sometimes it was by chasing people out of a pass seconds before an enormous avalanche came tumbling down on the area. At other times it was using his uncanny sense of smell to find and dig out people unlucky enough to be buried in an avalanche before they smothered to death.

Ever since his time the monks have had other St. Bernard dogs, all of them named Barry after that first dog who had a mysterious nose for danger. Today, if you pay a visit to Bern, Switzerland, you can still see Barry preserved and on display in that city's National museum. Because of his sixth sense, he is one of the few dogs to become a national hero.

One of the best stories about a dog's nose for

danger was uncovered by psychic expert Andrew MacKenzie. It involved a cocker spaniel named Merry and the Baines family who owned her and lived in a suburb of London during World War II. In those days London was a dangerous place to be in. Every week German planes flew over the city dropping tons of bombs on the English capital. Thousands of people were killed and maimed by the bombs and hundreds of homes were totally destroyed.

Like most who had to live with this danger, the Baines family had built an underground bomb shelter in their backyard in 1940, in the early days of the war. They would wait out bombing alerts in this little concrete room, which was equipped with bunk beds for Mr. and Mrs. Baines and their daughter, Audrey.

By 1944, four years later, the family had stopped using their concrete shelter because it always got too cold and damp and also because the bombs never seemed to fall dangerously close to their house. They decided to board up the entrance to the small underground room and instead use a specially designed steel table they had installed in their house. During the air raids they would huddle comfortably under it and not have to sit in the chilly damp shelter. For four years they used this table and never went out to their backyard shelter.

That changed one day when Mrs. Baines and her daughter were cleaning up some minor damage — cracked plaster and broken glass — caused by bomb shock waves. They had just finished the cleanup when they noticed their dog, Merry, was nowhere around. She wasn't in the house and wasn't in the backyard. There was no way she could have gotten away because a fence ran all around their property. Still, they couldn't find her and were starting to get worried.

Finally Audrey noticed in her search of the garden that one of the boards blocking the entrance to their old bomb shelter was knocked free. When she got a flashlight and looked inside she found Merry curled up on one of the bunk beds. It was a strange thing for the dog to do. In four years she had never wandered anywhere near the place before.

But today the dog seemed particularly attached to the damp, underground room. Three times Audrey and her mother chased the dog out. Three times the dog jumped back in, settling on Audrey's bed where she used to sleep during the long air raids. The third time, both mother and daughter went down to get the dog. While they were in the shelter they noticed how much more secure the place felt than the steel table in the house. Then Mrs. Baine said it was a shame they went to all the trouble of building the room and never used it anymore. On the spur of the moment she suggested they clean it out and sleep there that night just like old times. Once the dog saw the mother and daughter start cleaning up the shelter, she went off to play by herself.

By late afternoon the shelter was livable again

and that evening they settled in for their first night there in close to four years. While they slept, German planes flew over on a surprise bomb attack. One bomb slammed into the road right in front of the Baines house. It hit a gas main and turned the whole street into a river of flames. About half a dozen houses were destroyed in the explosion and fire, the Baines house among them. Knowing the family usually hid under their steel table, neighbors took one look at the pile of burning rubble where the house had been and gave up the whole family for dead. They were more than a little surprised to see the whole family, very much alive, later step up out of their backyard shelter followed by a cocker spaniel. Why the dog picked that particular day to make such a fuss about the bomb shelter wasn't very clear but no one bothered to complain.

Sea animals as well as those on land show a similar flair for making the right moves at the right time. Down in the fishing village of Eden in New South Wales, Australia, many of the villagers still talk about Old Tom, the killer whale. In the early 1900's whaling was still a prosperous business for the villagers of Eden and many of the old seamen came to know well a very special pack of killer whales that led them out for the day's hunt.

In the lead of this pack always ran a familiar whale the sailors nicknamed Old Tom. Every winter Tom and his pack would wait offshore for the men to take to their boats for a whale hunt. Then, acting like seagoing bloodhounds, the pack would lead the men to their prey, usually a gigantic humpback whale. Working together, they would drive it toward the whalers' boats and try to trap it in shallow water.

The pack would actually hold one of these enormous creatures in one place until the whalers got to it. Two killer whales would hold the large whale's tail still with their teeth while two others swam underneath to keep it from diving out of sight. The rest of the pack would throw their bodies at the whale's air hole forcing him to surface. That would be the seamen's clue to move in for the kill with their harpoons. The killer whales would eat what they wanted of the dead beast and leave the rest to the men. It was a good arrangement for both groups of hunters.

What was really remarkable is that sometimes Old Tom and his pack would go off hunting on their own. When they did trap a big one, two of the pack would then swim in to shore near the village and make loud slapping noises on the water with their fins. It didn't take long for the villagers to figure out that Old Tom and his pack had snared another whale for them.

Some people claimed all these stories about Old Tom were, to put it kindly, slightly exaggerated. Sure, killer whales were capable of hunting down and killing some of the biggest whales in the ocean, but the stories about the whales waiting for the fleet and leading them out to a kill did seem a little farfetched. People also didn't believe that one whale would have that much control over a pack.

The tales of Tom came to an end one morning in 1930 when the carcass of a killer whale washed up on the beach near Eden. The villagers recognized it right away as Old Tom. From that day on no killer whales were ever seen in the area again.

Another seagoing animal who was as famous as Old Tom was a porpoise who cruised the waters off the coast of New Zealand. Called Jack by the many sailors who saw him, the porpoise was especially fond of a treacherous waterway known as the French Pass. It was tremendously tricky to navigate and Jack made himself famous by guiding any ship he saw through the dangerous parts. As long as they followed his route through the channel the ships' captains knew they would be safe.

Jack's career as a channel guide almost ended one day. A drunken passenger on a ship called the *Penguin* thought the porpoise was a shark and fired his pistol at him. Two of the shots hit Jack and he sank beneath the water leaving a trail of blood behind. For a long time afterwards he wasn't seen and most people assumed the shots killed him.

A few months later Jack was back on the job. Miraculously he had survived his wounds and seemed as helpful as ever. As in the old days he acted as a channel guide for every ship he met but one, the *Penguin*. He never went near it again.

Jack was never able to get even with the man who shot him, though according to author John Train, some animals do. In his book *Remarkable Occurrences*, he says there was a man, hunting near Louisville, Kentucky, who shot and, he thought, killed a rabbit, which he picked up and stuffed into the game bag hanging from his shoulder. But the hunt wasn't over for the rabbit, which was still very much alive. Somehow it managed to wiggle out of the hunter's sack and get its paw on the trigger of the man's shotgun. The gun went off and shot the hunter in the foot. No one knows if the rabbit had a hunting license.

Sometimes it happens that even insects can get involved in coincidences, like the practical joke played on one woman by a grasshopper. It happened to the wife of the English writer J.B. Priestley. As a gift he bought her a collection of three small, handpainted pictures. She brought them up to their bedroom where she was planning to hang them up and piled them on a chair. The picture on the top of the pile, her favorite, was a drawing of a grasshopper.

That night as his wife climbed into bed, she felt something moving under the sheets. When she pulled back the covers she found a grasshopper skipping around. She picked it up and let it hop out the window. It wasn't until the next day that she realized just how odd her discovery was. In all the years she had lived in the house she had never seen a grasshopper anywhere indoors and certainly never found any skipping around her bed. And in the years since her discovery she never saw another.

Birds, other than pigeons, also figure in other people's coincidences such as one described by the famous psychologist Carl Gustav Jung. A woman he knew told him that whenever there was a death in her family, flocks of birds would gather on the house of the dying person. When both her mother and grandmother died, she said, birds settled on the windowsills of their bedrooms.

One day her husband went to a doctor complaining about pains in his chest. He thought something was wrong with his heart. The doctor examined him and told the man he was fine, not to worry. On the way home the man had a fatal heart attack and keeled over in the street. People who recognized the man picked him up and carried him home. They were surprised to see his wife standing in the door as though she were expecting them. When someone asked her why she had been waiting there like that, she simply pointed toward the roof of the house. A huge flock of birds had settled there.

What is probably the weirdest animal coincidence of all times happened to a man named Noel McCabe in England in 1974. He was relaxing at home listening to one of his favorite records called the "Cry of the Wild Goose." Just as he put on the record he heard a loud crash in his bedroom. He clicked on the light and saw that a Canadian Wild Goose had flown straight through his bedroom window. If that wasn't peculiar enough he then heard two thumps in his backyard. Two other wild geese had simply fallen there out of the sky. It was a long time before he played that record again.

6

Dreams of Coincidence

Do dreams *really* come true? Do things that happen in your dreams happen again in real life? Psychologist David Ryback didn't think so. Most people, he thought, would have a dream and only half-remember it the next morning. When they later saw a place or experienced something that was a little like their half-remembered dream, they'd be convinced they'd seen it all before. That's what Ryback used to think until he started looking more closely at what could be called coincidental dreams, ones which show you something that happens before it actually does. Then he realized the spooky fact that dreams *do* come true, at least for some people.

Of the many dreams he collected, one of the best was one told to him by a college student from Atlanta, Georgia. The young man dreamed he was in a bank, standing in line at a teller's window, when the doors flew open and two men carrying guns rushed in. One of the robbers walked over to the college student and stuck a gun in his mouth. The young man got out of the dream robbery the easiest possible way. He woke up.

The dream scared him so much he remembered it in all its details and described it to a friend he met the next day. Later that same day he had to go to his local bank on business and while he was standing off to one side of the main floor, two robbers came rushing through the bank's front doors. No one stuck a gun in his mouth, but his view of the robbery was the same one he had in his dream. Everything else happened as he saw it the night before. The only difference between this and his dream robbery was that he couldn't escape by waking up.

After collecting dozens of stories like this, Dr. Ryback is now convinced that for some people dream coincidences are very real. Now Ryback is studying dreams not to find out if they come true but why they do.

One thing experts do know about coincidental dreams is that they don't have to happen to you to come true. You can have these kinds of dreams about another person or place. This is what happened to J.W. Dunne, a British soldier who was stationed in South Africa in 1902. For years he kept having the same dream. He was always on an island and he always was standing on the lip of an enormous, active volcano in the middle of the island. It was a peculiar dream for him because he had never been on an island that was anything like the one in his dream and he had never seen a volcano except in pictures. One night in 1902 his old familiar dream changed slightly. As he was standing near its mouth, he knew it was going to erupt and smother the island in flaming lava.

He ran into the town at the base of the volcano and tried to warn the people. He went to the police station. He remembered the police were French. He also remembered they didn't seem to believe him. Dunne kept saying over and over again in his dream that unless they got everyone off the island, 4,000 people would be killed. Eventually people believed him and started getting ready to evacuate. But, as often happens in dreams of danger, everyone seemed to be moving so slowly.

Dunne never remembered how the dream ended, only the fear and panic that gripped him as he ran through his dream's village trying to warn people. He almost forgot about the dream until a few days later when he got the latest mail from England. In among the letters and packages was a week-old edition of a London newspaper, the *Daily Telegraph*. The headline story in that issue was about a volcanic eruption on the island of Martinique in the West Indies. The eruption came suddenly, viciously, without warning. Few people had a chance to escape. Entire villages were buried in molten lava and the last official estimate was that 40,000 people were killed.

When he checked the date of the disaster, he found that he had dreamed about it the night *after* it happened, but days before he ever got word of it. The other odd thing was that the real disaster turned out to be even worse than the one in his dream. His dream village lost 4,000 people. Martinique lost 40,000.

Bad news, death, and disaster seem to be what most coincidental dreams have in common. There are a few theories about why this is. One which is very popular now is that there is some kind of ESP at work. People who are dying or who are in real trouble sometimes send out psychic signals that the relaxed brain of a sleeper may sometimes pick up and interpret as a dream. Whatever the reason, some people do seem to see things in their dreams that they couldn't possibly know about.

The American Society for Psychical Research, an organization that studies such dreams, says it has in its files the case of a schoolteacher in Dallas, Texas, who had an unusual visitor one night. The teacher woke up (or maybe dreamed he awoke) in the middle of the night because he heard someone rattling the knob on his front door.

When he looked out he could see by the light of the street lamp that it was his father. He was surprised for two reasons. It was late at night, hardly the time for a surprise social visit from anyone. Stranger still was the fact that the late night visitor was his father. Both parents lived thousands of miles away in Los Angeles. What was he doing here in Dallas at this hour? Why didn't he call and say he was coming? the son wondered as he went to the door.

The father stepped into the room, shook his son's hand, and then walked out of the house, all without saying a word. The son looked out the front door and up and down the street after his father left but could see no trace of his visitor. All this may or may not have been a dream. The teacher was never really sure. He went back to bed.

What was no dream was the fact that a few minutes later the doorbell rang. It was a messenger with a telegram. It said that earlier that same evening the man's father had died in Los Angeles.

The teacher was totally confused. He was still convinced he had just seen his father and even described to his wife the clothes his father was wearing at the time they shook hands. When he later spoke to his mother he found out that those were in fact the very same clothes the father had on at the time he died. He never had another dream, if that's what it was, like that before or since.

Psychic experts at Stanford University uncovered two cases of similar dreams that involved someone else's death. The first happened in Chicago in 1894. One morning a young newspaper reporter named Arthur Pilbert was sitting at breakfast with his wife when she suddenly asked him if he knew of anyone by the name of Edsale or Esdale. He said no, and asked why she wanted to know.

During the night she said she had a bizarre dream. She found herself walking along the shoreline of Lake Michigan and saw a long box, lying near the water's edge. Going closer she realized it was a coffin with the lid nailed shut. On the lid was a small brass plaque with something engraved on it. She had to brush away some dirt to read it. Just one name was inscribed on it: Edsale or Esdale, she couldn't be sure about the spelling. It was such an odd dream it stuck in her mind when she awoke.

It didn't make any more sense to the husband than to his wife. He said it was probably just another nightmare, and went back to his paper. While reading local news he then came across an item he thought might interest her. There was a story about a police search going on it said for a missing man. His name was Edsale. A few days later the husband had another reason to think of his wife's dream. Another news story mentioned that the police finally found Mr. Edsale, lying dead on the shoreline of Lake Michigan.

The death image was not so obvious in the case of another woman's dream but the presence of it was unmistakable. A woman on vacation with her husband seemed disturbed as they were having breakfast in their room in the small New

England inn. She explained that she had dreamt about getting a letter addressed to her in unfamiliar handwriting. Without opening it she somehow knew that the letter was notifying her that she was being given $5000 and the only reason she was getting it was because a relative of hers had died.

The dream upset her because the only person who was likely to leave her money when he died was her brother. Even thinking about the possibility that he might be dying was disturbing.

Her husband tried to soothe her by pointing out that after all it was only a dream and probably meant nothing at all. Later that morning it was the husband's turn to be worried when he went to check on the mail and found a large envelope addressed to his wife. She took one look at it and said it was the same envelope she had seen in her dream. She couldn't bear to open it and asked her husband to do it for her.

He did and found a letter and a check inside. The check was for $5000. The letter, written by a lawyer from another part of the country, explained where it came from. A little over a year before an uncle whom she barely knew had died. In his will he asked that $5000 be left to this woman, his niece. It had taken the lawyer all that time to track her down to give her a share of the estate.

Most dreams of coincidence involve just the dreamer and one other person. Usually only the dreamer can see the dream. This was not the case with the strange dream of a Mrs. Wilmot. The year was 1863. Her husband had set sail from Limerick, Ireland, for New York City a few weeks before and now she heard his ship was in serious trouble. For more than a week it was caught in a vicious storm. No one knew when the storm would break or how much longer the ship could hold together.

Few people on board the ship got any rest during the storm, but when the storm did finally blow by, everyone took the chance to catch up on some of their lost sleep. Mr. Wilmot was one of them. Numb with exhaustion, he staggered down to the cabin he shared with another passenger. He toppled into the bottom bunk and was asleep in minutes. During his sleep he dreamt his wife walked into his cabin, kissed him lightly on the forehead, and left. When Wilmot woke up, the man who had been sleeping in the bunk above was looking at him very strangely.

He asked Wilmot who the mysterious woman was who came into the cabin. He added she was no one he remembered seeing anywhere on the ship. When Wilmot asked the man what she looked like, he described Mrs. Wilmot exactly as she appeared in the dream. Now Wilmot wasn't sure what was going on.

A little battered but in good shape, Wilmot's ship eventually made it to New York where he found his wife waiting. Shortly after he arrived she asked him jokingly if he remembered getting a visit from her while he was at sea. When he asked what she was talking about, she told him of a dream she had about three or four o'clock one morning as she lay half-awake worrying about how his ship was trapped in the storm.

She saw herself leaving her bedroom and drifting over the ocean until she saw his ship. She boarded it and found her way to her husband's cabin. When she saw that he was safe and fast asleep, she says she then dreamed she kissed him on the forehead, and that a man in the top bunk was staring at her.

When Wilmot asked her specific questions he saw that she was able to describe his cabin down to the smallest detail. Her story confused him more than ever. Now he wasn't sure if he was dreaming, if his wife was dreaming, if his fellow traveler was dreaming, or if all three were dreaming the same dream at the same time. The only other solution was that no one was dreaming and this really happened. But that was impossible. Or was it?

Because they are so close, husbands and wives are often much more sensitive to the good and bad things that can happen to each other. One woman, the wife of a Russian soldier, even dreamed in advance how and where her husband would die. The woman was the Countess Toutschkoff. Her husband, Count Toutschkoff, was an officer in the Russian army, which in 1812 was fighting Napoleon's army for the survival of Russia.

Three times that year the countess had the same dream. Each time, she was staying in the small room of a country inn located in a town she had never seen. During the dream her father came into her room, holding her small son by the hand. He said he had sad news. Her husband had been killed by the French. "He has fallen at Borodino," he said.

After dreaming this a third time she told it to her husband. He had never even heard of a place called Borodino. Curious about it, the two of them searched through dozens of maps of Russia trying to locate it, but were never able to find it.

Later that same year, 1812, the Russian army, after being driven back time after time, decided to stop retreating and make a last stand against the invading French Army. They drew up battle lines on the outskirts of a small village. Whoever won would rule Russia. The Russian army lost and the battle was a turning point of the war. It was named the Battle of Borodino after the village nearest to the fighting.

Count Toutschkoff and his troops fought in that battle while his wife and family stayed at an inn a short distance away. The Countess Toutschkoff waited nervously for news of who won the battle and how her husband did. Finally word did come. Her father entered the room where she waited. He was leading her small son by the hand. It was her dream come to life. Even before her father spoke, she knew what he was going to say.

Not every coincidental dream about the future is always about someone the dreamer knows. The same year the Russian countess was having her disturbing dreams about her husband's death, there was an Englishman named John Williams who was also having an equally strange dream, about a murder.

Williams was not by nature a dreamer. He was a hardheaded banker and engineer who usually had little patience for such nonsense. But even he couldn't ignore what he saw during his sleep. On the night of May 3, 1812, he dreamt he was standing in the hallway outside the House of Commons of British Parliament. There was a short man standing in the crowd that had gathered there. He was wearing a blue jacket and a white vest. It was an ordinary enough scene as dreams go until a tall man wearing a brown coat stepped up to the short man and shot him in the chest. People standing nearby grabbed the assassin. When Williams asked who had been shot, someone told him it was "the Chancellor."

The dream made such an impression on him that Williams found himself telling his friends and relatives about it in the days following. Then on May 11, a little over a week after his dream, there was a murder in the House of Parliament. A man named Spencer Perceval was standing in the hallway outside the House of Commons when another man named John Bellingham stepped up to Perceval and shot him twice in the chest.

Perceval died almost instantly from the shots. At the time of his death he was wearing a dark blue jacket and a white vest. Perceval was a successful politician with many titles. One of them was Chancellor of the Exchequer for the English government. It was no longer any mystery whose murder Williams had seen in his dream.

All coincidental dreams are not quite so grim. Psychologist C.G. Jung had a favorite story about one of his patients who was involved in an odd little coincidence. Jung was a believer in a theory that most coincidences followed a certain law, which involved a tremendous complicated set of rules. He was convinced that if we were able to figure out what the basic laws of coincidence were and how they worked, we would actually be able to predict when coincidences would happen, the way we now predict the weather. (Only he wanted to do a better job than the weatherman.)

Jung studied coincidences and collected them the way some people collect stamps, always looking for the one that would show the key to the laws he was convinced were there. He never discovered any laws, but he did get many people interested in the idea of coincidences, one of them a woman patient of his who didn't believe that such things happened. What changed her mind about the subject, of course, was a coincidence all her own.

She was visiting Jung one day, telling him about

an especially dazzling dream she'd had the night before. She had a kind of vague vision of someone giving her an exotic piece of jewelry, a solid hunk of pure gold carved in the shape of a scarab, a beetle that the ancient Egyptians often copied in their jewelry and designs. She couldn't remember who was handing her the present but she remembered the gift well, a small, delicate insect with the sheen of rich gold.

She had just finished telling Jung this story when he heard a buzzing and rattling on one of his window panes. A small flying bug was hurling itself against the glass as though it were trying to batter its way into the room. Jung opened the window to let it in and as it flew by he grabbed it out of the air. When he opened his hand he saw sitting there a beetle, a European scarab beetle to be exact. It had a greenish gold color to it like a fine piece of jewelry. He turned to his patient and held out his hand. "Here is your scarab," he said with a smile. From that day on she was a believer in coincidences.

Jung did know some other people who were already believers in coincidental dreams. Some even learned how to read them. One young man, a college student, was told by his father that if he did well on his exams, his reward would be a trip to Spain. The student told Jung he already knew he'd do well. When Jung asked him why he said that, the young man told him about a dream he had.

He saw himself in a foreign city strolling the streets. He could tell by its surroundings it was in Spain. He was walking at his own pace, turning down streets that appealed to him, when he found himself standing in a small square. An enormous old cathedral faced out on it. He studied it for a while, then turned right on another side street and saw standing in the street a beautiful carriage pulled by two elegant horses the color of cream. There his dream ended.

The student was right. He did do well on his tests and he got his trip to Spain. He had forgotten about his dream but was instantly reminded of it one day when he turned a street corner in Madrid and found himself standing in a small square. There was the old cathedral exactly as he remembered it, looking out on the square. He was about to step inside when he remembered the rest of his dream. He wanted to see if that was as accurate. He found the dream street where he remembered turning and walked down it. He had only gone a few steps when he saw it standing there, the same elegant carriage complete with the cream-colored horses.

Since we all seem to lead a whole other life in our dreams, at least in our dreams of coincidence, some people wonder if they can step inside their dreams. In her book, *Creative Dreaming*, dream expert Patricia Garfield describes how three Englishmen named Fox, Slade, and Elkington decided to try an experiment with something they called "dream travel." It was pretty simple. All you had to do was think of a specific place and, after you went to sleep at night, try to dream yourself there.

They got together and decided that on one particular night each of them would try to dream he was in a park they all knew called Southampton Commons. That night Fox dreamed he was strolling through a park. He was not surprised to see he was in Southampton Commons. During his dream walk who should he happen to meet but Slade, his fellow dreamer. The two men stood and talked for a while expecting their friend Elkington to show up. He never did. They made a little joke about this and each went his separate way through the dream park.

The next day Fox, wide awake, ran into Slade and told him about his dream and how they met. Slade mentioned that he had an almost identical dream in which he too saw Fox but no Elkington. Later on the two of them met Elkington who said that his experiment with dream travel was a big disappointment. He had tried to dream about the park but somehow just couldn't get there. And that, his other two friends claimed, is why Elkington was in neither dream. Or was it just a coincidence?

7

History Does Repeat Itself

Although the history books don't say too much about it, history is full of coincidences. Some are funny. Others are tragic. All of them are mysterious. In U.S. history the office of the presidency of the United States seems to have quite a few bizarre coincidences connected with it. One of them is the so-called 20-year curse on it that began in 1840. Every 20 years since then, whoever was president has never lived to complete his term of office.

President William Harris, elected in 1840, was the first to succumb to this curse, or odd coincidence (if you prefer). He died of pneumonia just a few weeks after his inauguration. The president who was elected in 1860, 20 years later, was Abraham Lincoln who of course was killed by John Wilkes Booth. In 1880 James Garfield was elected president and he was assassinated as well. William McKinley, who was elected in 1900, also died from an assassin's bullet. Warren

Harding died of an unknown illness after his election in 1920, and Franklin D. Roosevelt died of natural causes after his re-election in 1940. The next time the 20-year cycle came around was in 1960 when John F. Kennedy was president. He never completed his term of office either, but was murdered in 1963. The question now on some people's minds is: Is the 20-year curse over?

The eeriest set of coincidences ever connected with the presidency are those surrounding the murders of two of our country's most beloved presidents: Lincoln and Kennedy. Shortly after President Kennedy's assassination, peoples' thoughts naturally went back to other times in our country's history when a president was killed. And the more people talked, the more they began to draw up a long list of similarities between the two men and the people and circumstances surrounding their assassinations. These are some of the coincidences they uncovered.

Lincoln was elected president in 1860, exactly 14 years after he was first elected to Congress. Kennedy was elected president in 1960, 14 years after his first election to Congress. Each man's name had 15 letters in it. Each president had a vice-president who was a southerner, whose last name was Johnson, and who had 13 letters in his name. Lincoln's vice-president, Samuel Johnson, was born in 1808. Lyndon Johnson was born in 1908. The last name of Lincoln's personal secretary was Kennedy. President Kennedy's personal secretary was named Evelyn Lincoln.

Both men were shot and killed on a Friday. Both died of head wounds. Both died with their wives sitting at their sides. In each case the assassin was a southerner and each assassin, John Wilkes Booth and Lee Harvey Oswald, had 15 letters in his name. Neither man ever made it to trial but was killed beforehand. Finally, one minor coincidence: Lincoln was assassinated in Ford's theater, while Kennedy was killed while riding in a Lincoln car which is made by the Ford Motor Company.

Each president seemed to have a premonition about his death. A few days before his death, Lincoln had a disturbing dream in which he heard weeping and sobbing in the White House. He went to see what it was all about and eventually found a room with a coffin in it. Soldiers were guarding it and the room was filled with mourners. When he asked who was lying in the coffin, he was told, "The president. He was killed by an assassin."

Lincoln described this dream to a close friend who was so impressed he wrote it down shortly after he heard it. A few days later, on the day he was to die, Lincoln told his personal guard he was certain there were people who were determined to kill him and added, "If it is to be done, it is impossible to prevent it." On the day of his death, President Kennedy had also said to one of his personal advisors that anyone determined enough could easily take the life of the president of the United States. Both men, unfortunately, were right.

Once the presidents were buried there was one last small coincidence. After his father's funeral, Lincoln's son moved to a house in Georgetown, a section of Washington, D.C. The address was 3014 N. Street. John Kennedy's son also moved to a Georgetown house after his father's funeral. The address was also 3014 N. Street.

Another presidential coincidence has to do with two former presidents and a national holiday. John Adams and Thomas Jefferson, each of whom helped write and signed the Declaration of Independence, both died on the fourth of July, 1828, which also happened to be the 50th anniversary of the Declaration of Independence.

For other national leaders, a day, not a date, was what seemed to have a peculiar coincidence connected with it. Queen Victoria of England always became very nervous when Saturday rolled around. The reason was that so many of her relatives died on that day.

Her great-grandfather George II died on a Saturday as did her grandfather George III and her uncle George IV. Saturday was also the day on which her mother, her father, Prince Albert, and her daughter Princess Alice all died. One of her surviving relatives, her grandson Prince Albert Victor, was so worried about this coincidence that he never even went outside on a Saturday. As it turned out, neither the queen nor her grandson had anything to worry about. Victoria died on a Tuesday and her nervous grandson died on a Thursday.

With some people it's names and dates that seem to follow a certain pattern. Take the Bascomb family, for example. In 1895 a man from Illinois named James Bascomb was married on June 5. He and his wife eventually had a family of five children, four boys and a girl. The second-born child was a boy whom they called Eric W. Bascomb.

On another June 5, this one in 1924, that Eric W. Bascomb got married and in a few years started his own family. He also had five children, four boys and a girl and he gave his second-born child, a boy, the name Eric W. Bascomb, Jr.

Eric Bascomb, Jr. grew up and was married on (when else?) June 5, 1949, and had a happy, healthy family of five children: one girl, four boys. His second-born child was also a boy and the child was called Eric W. Bascomb III. The last time anyone had heard, Eric Bascomb III had no plans to marry, but when he does you can probably guess what date he'll choose for the wedding and what kind of a family he'll have.

Names by themselves also draw coincidences as one British playwright found out back in the 1940's. Writer Arthur Law came up with the idea for a play that was about a man who was the sole survivor of a shipwreck. He named the ship-wreck victim Robert Golding and the fictional ship that sank in the play he called the *Caroline*. The day he finished writing the play, Law was reading the paper when a small news item caught his eye. The story told about a ship that was caught in a sudden storm off the coast of England. The ship was totally destroyed and only one man survived the disaster. The ship's name was the *Caroline* and the sole survivor was a man named Robert Golding.

The all-time best shipwreck coincidence has to be the one mentioned in the *Book of Lists*. According to the book, on December 5, 1664, a ship carrying 81 passengers was caught in a storm in the Menai Strait, a channel of water off the coast of northern Wales, and sank. There was only one survivor, a man named Hugh Williams. On another December 5, this time in 1785, another ship carrying 60 passengers also sank in the same area. Only one person survived, a man named Hugh Williams. On a third December 5 in 1860, a ship with 25 passengers on it sank in the same area. Twenty-four of the passengers drowned. One was saved. His name, of course, was Hugh Williams.

Coincidences always seem to cluster around disasters for some reason, and one disaster case that had more than its share was the doomed British airship R101. In the 1930's, practically everyone believed that the real aircraft of the future was not the airplane but the dirigible, the airship, a gigantic version of what we know as the Goodyear Blimp. Airships could cover long distances easily and comfortably. Transatlantic flights were becoming more and more common. Traveling in airships was much more pleasant than traveling in cramped, noisy airplanes. Passengers slept in private cabins, ate in elaborate dining rooms, and at night could stroll the observation deck of the giant drifting aircraft to watch the earth moving slowly beneath them.

Airships were also faster than oceangoing ships. They used less fuel and they could carry tremendous loads because they were filled with the gas hydrogen, which was lighter than air; but it was this gas that eventually doomed all airships. Hydrogen was dangerous to use. One small spark could explode it into flames. Eventually scientists discovered a safer substitute gas, helium, which is used in the Goodyear Blimp today, but by then too many airships had burned up. No one was willing to fly in dirigibles anymore and the airship disappeared from the world's skies.

Attitudes were different in the 1930's. Germany, the United States, and England were all trying to outdo each other in building a bigger and better dirigible. England's entry in the airship race was an enormous one called R101. It was 777-feet long and was supposed to be the most advanced of its day. Even before it took its first flight, there were bad omens.

In 1925, five years before R101 was launched, Sir Stefon Brancker, and English official who would be one of R101's first passengers, was told by an astrologer that he couldn't find anything happening in the man's life beyond the year 1930. That was the year R101 was to make its first flight.

Eventually the giant, watermelon-shaped aircraft was built and a launch date was set: October 4, 1930. On the morning of that day, one of the crew members was leaving his home when his small son started to cry, "I haven't got a daddy." No one could calm him down, not even his father.

On the afternoon of that same day, the airship was launched on schedule. Its destination was India, but it was never going to make it. As R101 glided over France the weather kept getting worse. High winds roared against the airship, forcing it dangerously close to the ground. Many times the crew managed to pull it out of a dive. Eventually the winds won and the crew lost. At 2:05 on the morning of October 5, the huge dirigible smashed into the ground in a field in northern Franch and exploded. In seconds the ship was a ball of flame. Only six of the 54 people on board managed to escape. Sir Sefton and the crew member whose son was crying the day before were not among the survivors.

Strange stories connected with the disaster kept surfacing days afterwards. On October 5 at 2:05, the exact time of the crash, a Royal Air Force telephone operator heard a frantic clicking noise on the line connected to the office of Flight Lieutenant Carmichael Irwin. It was so suspicious someone actually went to see who was using the phone. There was no one there. Irwin was the captain of R101 and one of the many who died with it.

Three days after the disaster, a spiritualist said she had made contact with an R101 crew member while she was in a trance. He gave her a long list of technical defects in the airship, which he said helped caused the disaster. None of the defects were publicly known at that time and wouldn't be known until a year later when a special report was published. The spiritualist only managed to get part of her mysterious contact's name. It was Irwin.

Some of these stories can be explained away. It is possible that Sir Sefton had consulted an astrologer who couldn't plan more than five years into the future; and that the crewman's small boy was just very upset that his father was leaving him for a while. It probably wasn't very hard for the spiritualist to come up with Irwin's name. The papers were full of the news after the disaster and most certainly had mentioned the names of the prominent people on board. There are still the questions of how the spiritualist knew those secret, technical details and of the mysterious clicking telephone. Were they just strange coincidences or was Lieutenant Irwin somehow trying to warn the rest of the world?

Of all the disasters that have happened in history there is none that can equal the sinking of the ship *Titanic* for the number of baffling coincidences associated with it. That was one of the strangest and most tragic disasters in the 20th century. Even today it is still hard to believe such a thing actually happened.

To understand the tragedy you have to know a little bit about the ship itself. In 1912 the British had finished the ship *Titanic,* what was then the biggest, fastest, most luxurious, and, they claimed, the safest ocean liner ever built. Measuring over 800 feet long, it used the very latest in shipbuilding science.

One of most unique features about it was that it was built with a special double bottom lined with waterproof compartments. Even if something knocked a hole in its side, its builders said, the water would not reach the inside of the ship. The waterproof compartments would trap the water where it was and would keep the ship afloat. This, bragged the ship's designers, made the *Titanic* practically unsinkable.

On April 10, 1912, the brand new *Titanic* glided out of the port of Southampton, England, bound for New York City on her first voyage. No one who saw the huge ship leave that day would believe that just five days later, on April 15, the ship and over 1,500 of the people on it would be lying on the bottom of the North Atlantic. On that April night the ship was speeding through a stretch of ocean full of icebergs and sideswiped one of them, a giant, floating mountain of ice. It ripped a 300-foot long gash in the ship's side, big enough to start flooding all the waterproof compartments and eventually sink the unsinkable *Titanic.*

That collision was only the beginning of the disaster. When it was obvious the *Titanic* would sink, the captain gave the order to abandon ship. That's when the people on board had to face a second shock. Although the *Titanic* carried close to 3,000 people, her crew and passengers, she had lifeboats for only a little less than 2,000 people. For some reason the ship's designers didn't really think much about getting the people off, just in case their unsinkable ship should sink. Women and children were loaded in what lifeboats were available, and the husbands and fathers stayed behind to go down with the ship.

That didn't take long. It was shortly before midnight when the ship hit the iceberg. By two o'clock in the morning the front half of the ship was buried under water and the back half was sticking almost straight up in the air. All the lights in the ship had gone out and there was a sickening crash as the ship's engines tore loose from the back of the ship and dropped down into the front of the half-sunken vessel. Forty minutes later, at 2:40, the ship, with hundreds of people still clinging to it, sank to the bottom of the Atlantic. Ships in the area picked up the survivors, and when officials took a body count, they found over 1,500 had died mainly because the ship did not have enough lifeboats.

In the months and years that followed the tragedy, more and more stories surfaced, telling of amazing coincidences associated with the sinking of the giant ship. Most were the products of people's active imaginations, but a few were genuinely intriguing. One true story was told by a British businessman named J. Connon Middleton who had bought a ticket on the *Titanic*. About a week before he was to sail, he kept having the same dream over and over again. He saw a huge ship floating bottom up in the water with its panic-stricken crew and passengers swimming around it. The dream terrified him, and he began to dread the trip.

Then, about four days before he was due to leave, he got a telegram from New York, telling him to postpone coming for another week. He turned in his *Titanic* ticket and told his friends and relatives how relieved he felt. When they asked him why, he told them his dream. They said he was foolish to worry. He would have been sailing on the safest ship ever built. When the *Titanic* sank about a week later, they found out how wrong they were. It did not turn belly up before it sank as Middleton saw in his dream, but all the rest of his dream unfortunately came true.

Another person who never made it aboard the doomed ship was a sailor named Colin Mac-

Donald. He was offered a high-ranking job on the *Titanic*'s crew. It would have been a big promotion for him and would have earned him a lot more money. MacDonald said he was tempted by the offer but had some kind of vague feeling that the *Titanic* wasn't the ship for him. Three times he was offered the job. Three times he turned it down. The man who eventually got the position was one of the many who went down with the ship.

Others did sail on the ship, some in spite of warnings. The *Titanic* carried and killed many rich and famous people. One of them was a man named W.T. Snead, a noted British journalist. Although he often seemed to be predicting the *Titanic* disaster, he never paid attention to his own intuition. Once in the 1880's, years before the *Titanic* was built, he wrote a short story about a man who survived a shipwreck in which hundreds of people were killed because there weren't enough lifeboats. A few years later he wrote another shipwreck story, this one about a survivor who was rescued by a ship named the *Majestic*. At that time there really was a *Majestic* and the man in charge of it was a Captain Smith who later was to command the *Titanic*.

Snead even told an audience about a dream he had in which he was caught up in a mob of frantic people. He had the distinct feeling that he and everyone else in the mob was going to die a violent death. On April 10, 1912, he did.

The most famous of all *Titanic* coincidences was a novel entitled *Futility*. It was written in 1898, 14 years before the *Titanic* disaster, by a man named Morgan Robertson. It was the story about a giant luxury liner that sank after colliding with an iceberg. To make the sinking seem more dramatic, Robertson dreamed up a ship that was bigger and more powerful than any ship that existed in his day. It was a kind of supership of the 1800's. He described his make-believe ship in elaborate detail telling how long it was, how many propellers it had, and even how fast it was going when it hit the iceberg. Strangely enough his make-believe ship sounded like a twin of the *Titanic*.

Morgan's fictional ship was 800 feet long, was powered by three propellers, carried 24 lifeboats, and was traveling at a speed of 25 knots when it hit the iceberg. The *Titanic* was 880 feet long, carried 20 lifeboats, and was going at 25 knots at the time of its collision. The ship's designers in Robertson's novel also bragged how they had built an unsinkable ship. He added more drama to his shipwreck story by having his luxury liner run out of lifeboats before everyone got off. Also his fictional ship not only sank in April, the same month as the *Titanic* disaster, but it had an eerily similar name. It was called the *Titan*.

Years after the *Titanic* tragedy the coincidences continued. One now famous one happened in 1935 aboard a tramp steamer sailing through the

North Atlantic from England to Canada. It was just a few minutes before midnight, just about the time the *Titanic* struck that iceberg 23 years before. The young seaman on watch, William Reeves, noticed this and shivered slightly. At that moment he realized the ship was sailing in the same waters where the *Titanic* went down. It was also April, the month when that ship sank.

Reeves was not a superstitious man, but he had a spooky feeling something terrible was about to happen. He couldn't see very far out into the pitch dark night, but the sea was calm. Maybe he was just tired, he thought. It was near the end of his watch. Soon he'd be able to get some sleep. He had been working so hard that day he barely noticed what day it was.

Then it hit all at once. It was his birthday. He was born on April 10, 1912, the day of the *Titanic* disaster. There was something suspicious about all these coincidences happening at once: the fact that he, the only sailor on the ship, born on the day the *Titanic* sank, happened to be on watch on the same day, at the same time, and at the same place of the disaster. Without knowing why he shouted out a warning to stop the ship. The ship's helmsman threw the engines into reverse bringing the steamer to a dead halt in the water. That's when Reeves suddenly saw the shadow of an enormous hulk off to his right. His command had stopped the ship just a few dozen feet short of slamming into a gigantic iceberg.

Reeves' intuition had probably saved the lives of his fellow crew members and his ship, which by an odd coincidence was called the *Titanian*.

Not all of the *Titanic* coincidences are this fancy and this dramatic. One of the most recent ones, which happened in 1975, didn't happen at sea but in someone's house. According to a London newspaper, the Melkis family from an English town called Dunstable were sitting quietly at home one night watching a television movie about the sinking of the *Titanic*. Just as the film showed the boat crunching into the iceberg, their house shuddered as if a bomb had hit it. It turned out that a huge block of ice had fallen out of the sky and smashed through their roof. They were never able to figure out where the ice came from. The *Titanic* curse had struck again.

8

Good Luck, Bad Luck, Curses and Coincidence

Coincidence comes to us in many disguises. Luck is one of them. Most of us get our share of good and bad luck in about equal amounts. There are those who get more than a fair share of one or the other. There are some who have the kind of luck no person in his right mind would ever want. Like the lightning people.

There is an old saying that lightning never strikes twice in the same place, but you could never convince the Primardo family of that. With them lightning seems to be a family curse. It started in 1899 at the family home in Taranto, Italy. Grandfather Primardo was standing in his backyard when a bolt of lightning shot down from the sky and struck him dead where he stood. Thirty years later in 1929, his son was standing on the same spot during a storm. He was killed by a lightning bolt. In 1949, Rolla Primardo, the grandson of the first man and son of the second, apparently wasn't impressed by what happened to his ancestors. He stood in the same spot during a storm. He met the same fate when he too was hit by lightning.

Of course not all lightning people who have this kind of strange bad luck get killed instantly. One famous survivor was an Englishman named Major T. Summerford who was wounded in World War I, not by a bullet but by lightning. A bolt from the blue knocked him right off his horse. It killed the horse and temporarily paralyzed the major. A few years later, while still recovering from the first bolt, he was knocked down by a second. Lightning hit a tree near where he was standing, and the power of the blast blew him off his feet. He was paralyzed on his right side from the shock.

Two years after that, he had recovered from the first two blasts and was taking a stroll through a park in Vancouver, Canada, when a third bolt scored a direct hit. This was too much for his already weak heart. The Major died from his injuries. But his clashes with lightning didn't end there. One day during a sudden, freakish thunderstorm, a bolt of lightning snaked out of the sky and struck the ground in a cemetery in Vancouver, Canada. It hit one of the tombstones and shattered it. It was the stone marking the grave of Major Summerford.

If it's possible to be struck by lightning and still be considered lucky, Roy Sullivan, a forest ranger from Virginia, is the luckiest man alive. At last count he had been struck by lightning seven times and survived each jolt.

The first one happened in 1942 when a lightning bolt hit him in the foot. It knocked off his big toenail. Years later in July, 1969, bolt number two hit him and singed off his eyebrows. Bolt number three struck a year later in July, 1970, when lightning hit him and seared his shoulders. Number four came in 1972, when lightning struck him in the head and set his hair on fire. That made him a little nervous and he got in the habit of carrying a can of water in his car to put out the fire in case it happened again.

It did. In August, 1973, bolt number five shot out of a low-lying cloud and knocked him right out of his car so that he landed ten feet away. The lightning had gone right through his hat, set his hair on fire again, and traveled down his legs, blowing his left shoe off. He was slightly injured in July of 1976, when the sixth lightning bolt struck; and he had to be hospitalized for stomach and chest burns from lightning bolt number seven that hit him in June, 1977.

As a result of all this electricity, Roy Sullivan is a famous man. He is listed in the *Guinness Book of World Records* as the only man to have survived being struck by lightning seven times, and the scorched ranger hats he was wearing when he was hit are on display in the Guinness World Records Exhibits in New York City, Las Vegas, and Myrtle Beach. When asked why he keeps getting blasted by lightning, the only explanation he could offer was: "Some people are allergic to flowers. I'm allergic to lightning."

Although Roy Sullivan might not agree, most people think the number seven is lucky just as there are those who are sure that number 13 is unlucky. There are just as many people who are convinced that numbers are numbers. None of them is lucky or unlucky. There was once a group of men in London who called themselves the Eccentrics Club. They didn't believe in any superstitions. To prove how little they thought of them, they met once a month, on the 13th, and had a small party during which they did things like walk under ladders, break mirrors, open umbrellas indoors — all the things that are supposed to bring bad luck.

Just the same there are still a lot of people who aren't convinced. That is why, for example, you often won't see the 13th floor labeled in skyscrapers or why airlines often do not have seats numbered 13 on their planes.

If you want proof of the bad luck of number 13 at work, the believers say, all you have to do is look at what happened to the United States' attempt to land on the moon for a third time. Because of a defective spacecraft, astronauts James Lovell, Fred Haise, Jr., and John Swigart, Jr. weren't able to land on the moon and almost didn't make it back to Earth during a space moon mission back in April, 1970. And that was the only manned moon landing mission that wasn't successful. Its official name and number was Apollo 13.

If you take the time to notice, you will also see that no one on the Los Angeles Dodgers team wears the number 13 on his uniform. This was not always true. When the Dodgers were in Brooklyn there was a player named Ralph Branca, a pitcher who broke the superstitious tradition and wore the number 13. He was the first and the last Dodger player to do that. The reason, according to luck expert, author Max Gunther, is that just when he needed it most, Branca's pitching skill was suddenly jinxed, some say by his number.

Not many people were happy when Branca picked the number for his uniform in 1951. Many of his fellow players thought wearing an unlucky number was asking for trouble. Branca didn't agree and seemed to prove the number didn't matter by pitching well, at least at the beginning of the summer.

With his help the Dodgers had a good season in 1951. They made it all the way to the pennant playoffs for leadership in the National League. To get to the World Series they first had to beat their closest competition, the Giants.

In the deciding game, the Dodgers looked good. It was the last half of the ninth inning. The Giants were up at bat and had two men on base, but the Dodgers weren't worried. They had a comfortable lead and there were already two outs against the Giants. Their pitcher just had to deliver one more out and the National League Pennant was theirs. Ralph Branca was the pitcher.

Even the people who were at the game that day don't remember too clearly what happened. It looked like an easy win for the Dodgers. Some confident Dodger fans had already gotten up and were walking toward the parking lot to get a head start on the traffic. Giant Bobby Thompson, who wasn't an especially flashy hitter, was up at bat. The Dodgers had the game in the bag, they thought.

Branca wound up and threw the ball. Thompson cocked his bat and swung. He hit it. It was a home run, and the Giants won the game and the pennant. The fans going to the parking lot couldn't believe it. The sports announcers couldn't believe it. Ralph Branca couldn't believe it.

Some say the jinx of number 13 finally caught up with Branca. He didn't say that. He just said the ball felt kind of funny just before he threw it. Somehow he knew it was going to be a bad pitch. Officially, the Dodgers said nothing at all about Branca's unlucky number, but ever since that disastrous pitch in 1951, no Dodger ever wore number 13 again.

Thirteen is not the only unlucky number. There are people who seem to have their own jinxes or runs of bad luck attached to different digits. For Louis XVI, who was the king of France just before the French Revolution in the late 18th century, the jinx number seemed to be 21. When he was a child a court astrologer told him the 21st of any month was always going to be a bad day for him. The astrologer seemed to know what he was talking about.

Louis' first unlucky 21 came on June 21, 1770, when the king decided to make a grand entrance into Paris with his young queen, Marie Antoinette. The celebration was complete with fireworks, and an enormous crowd turned out to see the young royal couple. They followed Louis and his wife to a large plaza where they stood cheering for their king and queen. It was here that some of the fireworks went out of control, shooting straight into the crowd instead of up in the air. It caused a tremendous panic, sending people scrambling for safety. Over 1,200 people were trampled to death and 2,000 more were injured in the panic.

Exactly 21 years after that date, on June 21, 1791, the royal couple had another disastrous experience. They were arrested by the French revolutionaries and put in prison, and the following year on September 21, 1792, the revolutionary regime abolished royalty. The year after that Louis XVI saw his last unlucky 21. On January 21, 1793, he was executed on the guillotine.

Of course there are lucky numbers too. There is a popular one. Prince Otto von Bismarck, the famous German statesman and politician in the

19th century, lived a life that seemed to favor threes. Bismarck fought in and survived three wars. He served under three kings and signed three peace treaties. He had three children and owned three family estates. His family coat of arms was decorated with three clovers and it had the motto: "Strength in Threes."

Three was also a lucky number for a convicted English murderer named John Lee who became known as "the man they couldn't hang." Lee was sentenced to be executed by hanging but somehow the hangman just couldn't get the job done. Three times Lee was marched to the scaffolding and had the noose tightened around his neck. Three times the executioner pulled the lever that would drop the trapdoor under Lee. Each time the trapdoor stayed firmly shut.

No one ever figured out what the secret of his luck was. After each failure it was tested with a weighted dummy and it always worked fine. It never dropped for John Lee, however. After the third failure the authorities were so impressed by Lee's luck they changed his punishment from death to a prison term. He served his sentence and died a natural death years later.

Another person who had a similar run of luck with the number three was a convict in New South Wales, Australia, who was also condemned to be hanged. His name was Joseph Samuels and he kept claiming that he was innocent every time the authorities tried to hang him.

The first time they tried, the rope snapped. It happened again a second time. Finally they tried a new rope. This held but the weight of Samuel's body stretched it so that he was able to stand on the floor with his tiptoes and keep from choking. Fortunately for Samuels the police were still out investigating his crime and they found out that Samuels was right. He was innocent. He was released and they hung another man in his place.

People often discover their own lucky numbers in ways that are a little less drastic. Coincidence expert Arthur Koestler tells about how 23 became the lucky number for one woman. The woman, Mrs. Zeisl, lived in Vienna, Austria, as did most of her family. The family had more in common than living in the same city. Most of them, by a strange coincidence, all had the same address number on their home and business addresses. Her parents' house number was 23 as was her own. Her son lived at a house whose number was 23 and even his office number was 23.

On one of her vacations the woman was going to visit Monte Carlo in France where the internationally famous gambling casinos are. Although she never gambled, she joked that just once she might put a little money on 23 at the roulette wheel to see how it came out. The night before she went to the casino she was still trying to decide whether to gamble or not, but couldn't make up her mind. To distract herself, she picked up a book she had bought earlier that day and began reading. One of the characters in the book was a woman who had gone to a gambling casino, bet her money on 23, and won a huge amount of money. That's all Mrs. Zeisl needed to see. The following night she went straight to the roulette wheel. Like the woman in the novel, she put her money on 23, and like the fictional woman, she won.

One particular kind of luck that always fascinates is the bad luck of a jinx or curse. An old curse that some still believe in today is something called the evil eye. According to this superstition, there are certain people who are born with the ability to curse someone simply by looking at him. In some medieval courts the judges had criminals led into court backwards so they couldn't project the evil eye on them.

One person who is believed to have had the evil eye was King Alfonso who ruled Spain in the 1920's. The book *Strange Stories, Amazing Facts* tells of one incident that convinced several people he had this power. Alfonso was making an official visit to Italy in 1923 and was given a royal welcome by the Italian navy, complete with ships passing in review and 21-gun salutes.

One disaster after another kept happening at the welcoming ceremony. An old cannon fired to honor the king's visit exploded, killing those standing around it. One ship that sailed out to greet the king lost several crew members when a freak wave came out of nowhere and washed them overboard. Lastly, a high-ranking naval officer who was greeting the Spanish king shook Alfonso's hand, stepped off to one side to watch the rest of the greeting ceremonies, and abruptly dropped dead. Alfonso was never invited back.

Ships as well as people can carry around curses or jinxes with them. Most of the ship stories tell about ancient ships with their ghostly sails flapping in the night, but modern vessels have had their share of jinxes as well, if we can believe the story of U-65.

During the first World War the German navy built and sent off to sea many submarines, but none of them had the reputation of U-65. It seemed jinxed from the very beginning. During her very first dive, the submarine went out of control. Instead of leveling off under water it kept heading straight into the bottom of the ocean and was stuck there for more than half a day. The crew was about to suffocate to death when U-65 suddenly broke free and surfaced.

Problems continued even on shore. One of her torpedoes mysteriously detonated while being loaded inside of her. Six crew members including one of the ship's officers, a second lieutenant, were killed. After this even stranger things started happening.

Different crew members began seeing the dead lieutenant. One sailor swore he saw the officer late one night. He said the man was standing at the front of the boat with his arms crossed, staring out to sea. Another crew member said he saw the officer appear briefly on deck, then step off the side of the boat into the ocean and totally disappear. A third sailor was so terrified at having seen the dead man wandering around the sub that he jumped ship at the first port they visited.

More deaths followed. While the submarine was docked for repairs, its captain was killed by a stray bomb fragment during an enemy air attack on the harbor. During the first patrol after this, one crew member hung himself and another went mad for no apparent reason. By that time U-65 had the reputation of being a good submarine to avoid among German sailors.

The mysterious jinx and the war career of U-65 ended suddenly on July 10, 1918, off the coast of Ireland. An American submarine spotted the German craft drifting along aimlessly and decided to close in for the kill. Before the Americans could fire a shot, U-65 was torn apart by an enormous explosion from somewhere inside of it. It sank within seconds, leaving behind some pieces of debris, but no survivors. The last thing seen before it sank was the peculiar sight of one lone sailor with his arms crossed, standing at the front of the submarine looking out to sea. He appeared to be a German naval officer, a second lieutenant.

When it comes to curses and jinxes, the prize for the best series of weird coincidences would have to go to what is sometimes called the curse of King Tut. After lying hidden and undiscovered for 3,300 years, the burial chamber of the 18-year-old Pharaoh Tutankhamen was finally discovered in 1922 by a British archaeologist named Howard Carter. He had spent 25 years of his life and over a half million dollars loaned to him by a rich British aristocrat named Lord Carnarvon looking for Tut. On November 2, 1922, Carter sent Carnarvon a telegram saying the search was over. He had uncovered the boy king's tomb and it was in perfect condition. A little over two weeks later, November 26, Lord Carnarvon was at Carter's side as he broke the seal on the door to the perfectly preserved tomb. It was like stepping into a time capsule and traveling backwards over 30 centuries.

What they found was a dazzling collection of Egyptian art, rare archaeological relics, and whole statues carved out of gold — and all undisturbed. Most spectacular of all was the coffin that held the body of the young king. It was made of the purest gold and weighed close to 300 pounds. Fitted over the mummified head of the king was a funeral mask carved in the king's image. It too was solid gold and weighed over 20 pounds. There was so much in the tomb that it took Carter and his helpers over ten years to photograph all the items and remove them to a museum.

When the story of the curse began no one is really certain. Workers who were there the day the tomb was entered say that was when the first of many strange things happened. As the last person climbed up out of the opened tomb a sudden sandstorm hovered over the opening of the tomb and just as quickly disappeared. As the cloud of sand faded away, one of the workers pointed to the sky. There was a lone hawk, the symbol of the pharaohs, flying west, the direction of "the other world," according to ancient Egyptian beliefs. Some Egyptians said this was a sign that the spirit of the pharaoh had abandoned his tomb and left a curse behind on those who had disturbed it.

Another story about the curse began with a different kind of omen, the death of a canary. At the time Howard Carter opened the door to the tomb he found standing guard on either side of the doorway human-sized statues of the king. Each figure was wearing a crown with a golden cobra, the serpent god of the pharaoh, perched on it in a striking position. Carter would have another meeting with the cobra god a few days later.

He had a pet canary who often was his only companion on those lonely nights in the desert when he was searching for Tut's tomb. That bird was very special to him. A few days after he had broken the tomb's seal, he heard a tremendous amount of commotion around the tomb entrance. When he went to see what was going on, he found that a cobra had gotten hold of his pet canary, dragged it to the door of the tomb, and killed it there. Carter said it was an accident. Some of his workers said it was a warning from Tut and walked off the job.

Work went on in spite of the omens, and when Carter examined the lid on Tut's coffin, he found what some say is the actual curse of Tut written out. Part of it says: "Let the hand raised against my form be withered! Let them be destroyed who attack my name, my foundations, my effigies, the images unto me."

Whether there actually was a curse and whether it worked is still a matter of opinion. One thing that is true is that there was a strange series of deadly coincidences that happened shortly after Carter began cleaning out Tut's tomb. Many of the people who worked with him or who just paid a visit to the tomb while it was being emptied died under mysterious circumstances.

The list of casualties is long enough to make you think maybe there was a curse. One of the first to go was Lord Carnarvon himself. He never lived to see the gold coffin of the young king opened. A few months after the discovery he died in Cairo from an infected mosquito bite he got while visiting the tomb. At the precise moment he died, 1:55 in the morning, all the lights in the city of Cairo went out. At that same time at his family estate in England his pet dog gave out one long howl and then dropped dead on the spot.

When Lord Carnarvon's half-brother, Colonel Aubrey Herbert, visited the tomb, he is supposed to have said, "I feel something dreadful will happen to our family." A few years later he himself died of what doctors had thought was just a mild cold.

Another man connected to Carter's expedition was a wealthy businessman named Joel Woolf who had also given Carter money to finance his search. He too visited the tomb and shortly afterwards disappeared from his yacht, which he had docked in the Nile. A few days later his body was discovered floating in the river.

Two descendants of the pharaoh, Prince Ali Farmy Bey and his brother, both died violently after visiting the tomb. The prince was murdered in his hotel room in London and the brother committed suicide.

The curse or whatever it was got to other visitors of the tomb as well. Sir Lee Stack, a British official from the area, came by to inspect the tomb. A short time later he was assassinated. American millionaire George Jay Gould stopped by the tomb to have a look and while he was there suddenly became sick. A little while later, he died in France of whatever that mysterious "tomb" illness was. Finally, another visitor to the tomb, a wealthy woman named Evelyn Greely, shot and killed herself shortly after she saw Tut's treasure.

Those who worked with Carter on the excavation met with equally curious fates. A British archaeologist who was helping Carter study and catalogue all the treasures was killed in an automobile accident. Richard Bethell, who was the son of a Lord Westbury, worked as Carter's secretary for a while. Once he returned to London, he died mysteriously in his bed. Some say it might have been suicide, but doctors said whatever it was, it wasn't a natural death. A few months after his son's death, Lord Westbury killed himself. He jumped from the window of his London apartment, which was filled with Egyptian relics. He left behind a suicide note that said mysteriously. "I cannot stand any more horrors."

If there was a curse at work, it missed one very important person. When you look over the names of all those who died mysteriously, you'll notice that one person is missing: Howard Carter. Nothing weird ever happened to him except for losing his canary. He never went mad or became mysteriously ill and did not die in any horrible or unusual way. He lived a long, satisfying life and died peacefully in his sleep in his small cottage in England.

If there really was a curse, why didn't it strike Carter the way it did everyone else? After all, he was the one who was most responsible for finding and opening the tomb. If there was *no* curse, then why did so many people connected with Tut's tomb die so mysteriously? For that question there is only one answer: it was pure coincidence.

9

The Psychic Secret of Coincidence

Alex Tanous is a man who has lived with coincidence all his life. Unlike some people who sometimes wonder why coincidences happen, he knows the reason. He is gifted with extrasensory perception, ESP for short, which he says has given him the psychic ability to know in advance when some things are about to happen. It is a talent he says he inherited from his mother.

In his book *Beyond Coincidence*, he describes a strange incident in which his mother's talent saved his life and his brother's. At the time the Tanous family was living in a second floor apartment, which had a stairway in the front and in the back of the house. One day Tanous and his brother were going out to play and were about to run out the front door and down the stairs when their mother shouted, "No! Don't go that way!" Startled but obedient the boys turned around and headed for the back door, wondering why their mother was so particular.

They had barely gotten there when they heard a loud crash from the front of the house. The wooden stairs there had suddenly pulled away from the building and collapsed. When the boys asked their mother how she knew the stairs were going to collapse, she said she really didn't know. She just had a vague feeling something bad would happen to them if they went out that way.

Tanous himself came to have these same kinds of feelings. Once when he was still a young boy he had warned a man against driving over a certain railway crossing. The man ignored the boy's warning and a short time later he died. His car was hit by a train at that same crossing.

This kind of thing continued to happen to Tanous when he got older. At one time when he was working as a disc jockey, he announced that the record he was about to play was by the late (meaning dead) Hank Williams, a popular country and western star. It was a strange slip of the tongue because Williams was very much alive at the time. It also turned out to be a prophetic slip of the tongue because just a few weeks later, Hank Williams suddenly died.

How did Tanous know these things? Some experts now believe it is not too farfetched to say that ESP is behind some of what we see as coincidences. Just as there are people who have a certain talent for sports or playing musical instruments, there are those who seem to be born with a knack for ESP. Just how many people have this talent, no one is sure. It depends on the experts you ask.

Psychiatrist Dr. David Loye who teaches at the University of California believes that practically everyone has some kind of special talent for one bizarre feat, predicting the future. He calls this skill the gift of prophecy. Although there have been many crackpots who have made similar claims, Loye is taken seriously. Not everyone believes him but he has come up with enough evidence to make people wonder.

Some of his proof goes back to an experiment done in the 1930's by a Dr. Douglas McGregor at the Massachusetts Institute of Technology in Boston. McGregor was wondering how people made predictions about the future. He basically just wanted to know if they tried to figure out what the future would be like based on what they knew or if they just took wild guesses. He gave 400 people a list of future possibilities and asked them to make predictions. Most, he found, made wild guesses, but the predictions were so far in the future that McGregor had no way of knowing how good or bad they were.

Loye dug up McGregor's test answers years later and found out the predictions were pretty good. In four out of five cases the people guessed right about things they could not have known in advance. McGregor's people predicted there would be another world war (World War II); that it would start when Germany invaded Poland;

and that Germany would be one of the losers at the war's end. The people even were able to predict how the sides would be drawn: Germany, Italy, and Japan against the U.S., England, France, and Russia. At the time the people were asked the questions, there was no way they could have possibly known about these events. All they could do was guess. Their guessing, says Loye, brought out their talents for prophecy.

Two other people who seemed to have this knack, Loye says, were President John Quincy Adams and one of his grandsons, Henry Adams. In 1843, after he had left the presidency, John Quincy Adams wrote to a friend saying that he sensed that in less than 20 years there would be a terrible war that would divide the country. And it was in 1861, 17 years after he made this prediction, that the Civil War broke out.

His grandson Henry, who became a famous historian, also made his share of predictions. He said in an essay written in the late 1800's that around 1917 there would be a tremendous upset in world power. This eventually came true as World War I. He also said that some time in the 20th century most of the power in the world would be divided between two countries, the United States and Russia. At the time he wrote this, most people thought he was crazy. France, Germany, and England were the major countries of the world and many believed they'd stay that way for centuries to come.

Finally, he made what some say is his most dazzling prediction: that man would figure out how to take the power of the atom and make powerful weapons from it. At the time Adams wrote this there wasn't even electric power much less atomic power. How did he know we would have the atomic bomb?

Loye would say that all Adams did was use his natural power of prophecy. If Loye is right in saying we all have this future vision, his theory could explain the surprising results of a future test a teacher gave in the 1950's.

Richard Auerbach was a teacher of the fifth grade at the Eggert Road Elementary School in Buffalo, New York, in 1953. He wanted to get his students interested in writing essays, and, as one assignment, asked them to predict what the world would be like in 25 years, in 1978 to be exact. When all the essays were turned in, he told the class he was going to put them in his own private time capsule, a large envelope that he sealed with tape, and that he wouldn't open it until 25 years from then, in November, 1978.

The 25 years passed and Auerbach kept his word about not opening the envelope, although he said now and then he did feel tempted to take a peek. In November, 1978, he pulled out the papers and started reading. There were some wrong predictions but what surprised him were so many right ones.

One girl said that in 1978 practically everyone in the country would own a color television set.

This was an uncanny prediction because in 1953, at the time she wrote the essay, color television didn't even exist except as a few experimental models in laboratories.

Another student who had his mind on space predicted we would send rocket ships to the Moon, Venus, and Mars, which, of course, we have done. When he was making this prediction no one had been able to send rocket ships anywhere. In 1953 men hadn't even managed to get a satellite into orbit. The first satellite wasn't launched until 1957, four years later. Except for some science fiction writers and one or two wild-eyed scientists, few people thought we'd be able to send rockets to space until the very end of the century.

Other amazing predictions Auerbach found in his time capsule were: that we would have a camera that could develop the film inside itself and hand the picture to you; and that we would be zipping back and forth across the Atlantic Ocean in less than three hours aboard planes that flew faster than the speed of sound. (We now do that with the SST.) There are really only two ways you can explain predictions like these. Either Auerbach's fifth grade class were really lucky with their guesses or they were using without realizing it what Dr. Loye calls the gift of prophecy.

There was one man who used his gift to make a small fortune for himself. His name was Jesse Livermore and he made his money buying and selling shares of stock on the New York Stock Market.

Trying to make money on the stock market is a little like gambling. What everyone wants to do is buy shares in a company that will keep making more money. This way you could buy a share for five dollars one month and see it worth 20 dollars a few months later. If you wanted to, you could sell that share for 20 dollars and make a nice profit. Of course the stock market goes the other way as well. You could buy a share for five dollars and a few months later it could only be worth 50 cents. That's all you could get for it. The tricky part about the stock market is that companies can suddenly make money and just as suddenly lose it.

Jesse Livermore became famous for being able to sense the right time for buying stocks in a company and the right times for selling it. He made millions doing it. His most famous move was one day in 1906 when he suddenly decided to sell off his shares in the Union Pacific Railroad Company, which then was one of the richest businesses in the country. Other investors thought poor Jesse's mind had finally snapped. If there was ever a company bound to get richer, it was Union Pacific. They were convinced he was crazy when they asked him why he decided to sell his shares. He said he didn't know. He just had a feeling he should get rid of them.

Just a few days later word reached the East

coast of a terrible disaster. The city of San Francisco had been wiped out in an earthquake on April 18. Among other things buried in the rubble of the burning city were millions of dollars worth of equipment belonging to Union Pacific. That rich company suddenly was poor. The value of its stock became practically worthless. Everyone who had shares in it lost thousands of dollars. Everyone but Jesse Livermore. By selling his stock when he did he saved himself from losing over $300,000.

Not everyone who has the gift of seeing the future uses it to get rich. In the little town of Petrich in Yugoslavia there lives an elderly blind woman named Vanga Dimitrova who uses her powers to help those who need it the most. According to psychic experts Sheila Ostrander and Lynn Schroeder, who wrote about Vanga in their book *Psychic Discoveries Behind the Iron Curtain*, she found her ability to see into the future on the day when she was told she would go blind.

Vanga had been losing her eyesight steadily since she was a little girl. Different operations were tried but none seemed to do any good. When she was 19 years old and still able to see a little, her father took her to some more doctors. They said they could save her eyesight with a very expensive operation. The father, who was a poor farm worker, said he couldn't afford it. In that case, the doctors said, Vanga would go blind.

The day she came home from the hospital

Vanga told her sisters she had a horrible feeling that their father would die soon. They told her she was just upset about her bad news and to forget about her prediction.

Vanga turned out to be right. A few weeks later her father did die unexpectedly. After that other predictions followed. When they started to come true, Vanga's family and friends thought her being right about future events was just a coincidence; but when she kept on making true predictions year after year, they knew it was not just a matter of making lucky guesses. Somehow Vanga could sense the future.

When her brothers went off to fight against the Germans in World War II, for example, she told one of them he would die when he was 23 years old. He laughed and said he would live to be an old man. Vanga was right. About a year later he was captured by Nazi troops and shot by a firing squad. The day he was executed was also his birthday. He just turned 23 that day.

Gradually word got around about Vanga and her amazing gift of seeing into the future. People began making trips to her house asking about missing friends and relatives. One neighbor, a local farmer named Boris Gurov wanted to know what happened to his brother. He had disappeared over 20 years before when he was only 15. No one in the family had heard from him since.

Vanga told Gurov his brother had become a

Russian scientist but at the moment was being held as a prisoner by the Germans in a concentration camp. She added that this brother would be coming home the next spring. Gurov would recognize him by the fact that the brother would be wearing a gray suit and be carrying two suitcases.

Gurov said it sounded like a nice fairy tale but he didn't believe it. He didn't believe his brother was still alive much less that he had become a scientist. When he got home he told his family Vanga's story complete with the details about the suit and suitcases. Then he forgot about it.

It came back to him quickly enough one day the following spring when a stranger showed up in his front yard. It was a man carrying two battered suitcases and wearing a gray uniform. The man said he was Gurov's long missing brother, Nicola. He had run away to Russia where he eventually went to school and became a successful engineer. When war broke out between Russia and Germany, he joined the army. He was captured by German troops, held in a prison camp, and later released. Still wearing his gray prison uniform Nicola decided to go home.

Vanga once even used her powers to solve a murder that no one knew had been committed. A woman came to her and asked her questions about her sister who had died a mysterious death 15 years before. Vanga said the woman had actually been murdered by her husband who set up a fake alibi for himself, making it look as though he were in another city at the time he killed his wife. Not long after, the man confessed to the murder.

Vanga was never able to explain how she managed these feats. It was a power, she said, that seemed to appear on its own. There were times when she wasn't able to answer anyone's questions and there were also times when some of her answers were wrong. But, according to scientists who have studied her closely, on the average four out of five predictions turned out to be correct. As yet no scientist has been able to figure out why she is right so much of the time.

There are other types of ESP powers that may be behind what people consider coincidences. In his study of coincidence, expert Arthur Koestler came across a case of some strange happenings in what seemed to be a case of mind over matter. The weird events began in the summer of 1967 in the office of a lawyer named Sigmund Adam who worked in the town of Rosenheim, Bavaria. The troubles started with the telephone switchboard. Calls kept getting mysteriously disconnected. Telephone lines would mysteriously switch off and on with no one talking on them. The switchboard was recording phone calls that no one made.

At first the solution seemed simple. Complain to the phone company and get a new switchboard. Mr. Adam did, and got a brand new switchboard, which did as many weird things as the first. After months of problems, the lawyer thought someone was deliberately tampering with the equipment. He called in the police.

When the detectives arrived, other strange things began going on. Fluorescent bulbs kept burning out day after day. Each time one went it gave off a loud pop. Then light bulbs that weren't even switched on began exploding. Light fixtures started swinging mysteriously. Fuses were constantly blowing out.

Each time something new would happen, the police managed to come up with plausible explanations, such as poor wiring or overloaded circuits. After a while they started running out of explanations. Pictures that were hanging on the wall started spinning around. (Detectives took a videotape of one as it was twirling.) Others slid off their hooks and dropped to the floor. A heavy filing cabinet that weighed at least 400 pounds slid across the floor, all by itself. It was then that the police called in some scientists.

One of them, an ESP expert named Dr. Hans Bender, noticed that by an odd coincidence these things only happened when one person in particular was in the room. She was Mr. Adam's 18-year-old secretary, Annemarie. Bender found out that she had a crush on her boss. He also guessed that by using some psychic power she was causing all these strange problems with the telephones, the lights, and the other spinning, sliding office fixtures because she was upset with her boss and mad at the police for poking around. Bender suggested to Annemarie's boss that he let her go and she should get another job.

It seemed like a strange solution to his problems but since nothing else seemed to work, Adam tried it. The day after Annemarie left, all the weird occurrences stopped for good. Problems didn't stop for her, however. She never learned to control her psychic power when she got mad.

Annemarie found another job and a boyfriend whom she liked very much. They did have one problem. He loved bowling and she hated bowling. Just how much she hated it, the boyfriend found out when he insisted on taking her with him on bowling dates.

On at least eight dates with her he couldn't bowl because the electronic pin-setting equipment kept breaking down. At first he thought it was just a coincidence that it only happened when Annemarie was around. It wasn't long before he figured out that Annemarie was doing something to the bowling machines when she showed up, *what* he didn't know. Finally there was a showdown between the two of them. She said she wouldn't leave the machines alone and that he either had to give up bowling or give up her. The last anyone heard, she was looking for a new boyfriend, one who didn't bowl.